Ready...
Set...
Go!

Individual Counseling

School-wide Programs

Career Development

Peer Mediation

Small Groups

Parent Support

A Practical Resource for Elementary Counselors

By Janet M. Bender, M.Ed.

Classroom Guidance Lessons!
Reproducible Forms!
Time Management!
Self-Care Materials!

© 2003, 1999 by
YouthLight, Inc.
Chapin, SC 29036

Reprint and Cover Design by Elaine Callahan
Layout by Martha Stroud and Elizabeth Madden
Project Supervisor - Elizabeth Madden
Project Editing - Susan Bowman

ISBN 1-889636-47-9

Library of Congress
2002111763

10 9 8 7 6 5 4 3 2 1
Printed in the United States of America

YouthLight, Inc.
P.O. Box 115
Chapin, South Carolina 29036
(800) 209-9774 • (803) 345-1070
Fax (803) 345-0888 • Email YL@sc.rr.com

Dedication

To all the school counselors who work tirelessly
to make this world a safer and more caring place for children.

"It is better to build children than to repair adults."

Anonymous

Acknowledgments

I would like to thank the following people for their contributions to this book:

To God for blessing me with the ability and insight to write and for giving me the courage to risk in this venture.

To my daughter Amy and my wonderful husband Frank whose love and support encouraged me on this journey.

To my parents, James and Lenore McAlpine, who nurtured me so that I might nurture others.

To Dr. Charlotte Murrow Taylor, who was my supervisor and mentor when I was a new counselor.

To all the school administrators who allowed me the professional trust and freedom to grow.

To the practicum students I have supervised who inspired me to create this book.

To my fellow counselors in Berkeley and Dorchester counties who have taught me so much through the years.

To Dr. Bob Bowman for having confidence in me and guiding the organization of this book.

To Dr. Michael Kollar whose guidance and counseling has modeled the best of what a counselor should be and helped me discover my best self.

Table of Contents

Chapter 8:   A Pitstop at the Rest Area
(Taking Care of the Caretaker)......................................175

Appendix 185

Introduction

As one of the pioneer elementary counselors in Berkeley County, SC in 1981, I was grateful to have a district guidance coordinator to mentor and guide me in setting up my program. Still, working part-time at two schools - an elementary and a middle school - made it a challenge to say the least. I learned many things through the "school of hard knocks."

Ten years as a classroom teacher in first through third grades, gave me valuable experience in working with students and parents, but the shift to the counselor role was a whole new career journey. Even with the leadership of a district coordinator, I had to explore and learn for myself how to balance being a successful counselor with being a healthy individual. In a profession founded on caring and service to others, counselors are especially prone to "burnout." It took close examination of myself, my program, and my goals in life to come to the awareness of how to maintain a healthy balance among mental, physical, emotional, and spiritual realms of my life. I believe in counseling—-professionally and personally. My path to becoming a strong counselor for children included counseling for myself along the way. Someone once said, "You can't give what you don't have." I live by this belief.

Over the past 18 years, I have had the pleasure of supervising four counselors-in-training through their practicum experiences. I have also worked alone and with three different partners in three schools. This book is written in response to a perceived need I see in the counselor preparation process. I believe it can provide a "bridge" for new counselors from graduate school to elementary school. I hope it will also be helpful to experienced counselors looking for new organizational strategies and tips to maximize their efficiency and prevent burnout.

This book is not intended to tell you everything you'll ever need to know about school counseling. There are already several well written research-based guides of that type such as: A Survival Guide for the Elementary/Middle School Counselor, John J. Schmidt, and The School Counselor's Book of Lists, Dorothy J. Blum. This book is to be an experience-based quick reference "driver's manual" of sorts for the busy counselor who may feel overwhelmed by the enormity of the responsibilities ahead of him/her.

The first three chapters of this guide will help the counselor plan and prepare for the yearly journey before commencing. Chapter 1, Getting Ready, outlines steps to take before the students arrive. Chapter 2, Get Set, gives you a warm up period for the first two weeks of school. Chapter 3, Go, gets you going at full speed into your program. Chapters 4 through 7 detail basic strategies for organizing and working with individuals, small groups, classroom guidance, and school-wide programs. The final chapter is devoted to self care for the counselor.

Just as with your car, regular preventive maintenance and refueling along the way is essential for going the distance in this career.

Throughout this guide, I will refer to cautions along your journey or potholes to avoid. Each chapter includes forms and activities that pertain to information in that chapter. Feel free to use or adapt them to suit your needs. At the end of each chapter is a review of Points to Remember for quick reference and review. Additional resources and references are cited at the end of the guide.

I hope the journey will be as exciting and rewarding for each of you as it has been for me. Thank you for letting me share my experiences with you.

– Janet M. Bender

CHAPTER 1

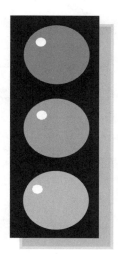

Getting Ready
(Before School Starts)

Congratulations, you've landed a job as an elementary school counselor! Now what do you do? You may have many years of experience as a classroom teacher, but you feel like a 15-year old about to take your driver's test. Don't panic! You're about to begin an exciting and rewarding journey. There will be many times when you must search for your own path, but I hope this book will serve as a road map to help you find your way and avoid common potholes along the way.

Transition in Roles

Experience as a classroom teacher is extremely valuable to you as a new counselor. It allows you to feel comfortable teaching a large group of students and gives you practice in dealing with parents. If you have not had classroom experience, you can still be an effective counselor. It may, however, take some time and practice to feel confident in front of a class. In either case, the school counselor wears a different hat from that of the classroom teacher in several ways.

To be an effective school counselor, you must make a successful transition from disciplinarian to **facilitator**. In some ways, all adults in the school setting are looked upon as authority figures. The counselor's role lies somewhere in "no man's land." You will have more responsibility and authority in the main office area, but at the same time you will need to align yourself as an adult friend and helper for the students. The counselor's office or room should never be viewed by students as a place one goes when "in trouble." It should be a haven for the students — a place where they can express their feelings and opinions openly and honestly without fear of negative consequences. If a child is reprimanded, scolded, judged or punished as a result of a visit to the counselor's office, he will not likely be back to reveal confidential, personal concerns. Ideally, the student should leave the counselor's office willing and eager to return to this friendly, inviting and safe place. Establishing rapport and trust is a must!

Establishing this role as facilitator of learning and growth takes time and practice. It does not come naturally upon obtaining a degree in counseling, but maintaining an awareness of your changing role is a good start toward achieving this goal.

What about your role in relationship to the teachers and other support staff? That, too, will be different. It is natural for classroom teachers to view the counselor's position as a promotion from classroom to "ivory tower." After all, you have your own office and telephone (hopefully). You have the freedom to set your own schedule. You can go to the rest room anytime you wish. You may have input into administrative decisions. You sit in your office, sip coffee and talk on the telephone all day. Right!!

Your relationship with the classroom teacher is vital to the success of the total guidance program. Teachers can be your greatest advocates or your worst critics—and be prepared for some of both. You won't be able to please everyone all the time, but when it comes to staff relations, communication is your ticket to success. Teachers need to know that you are busy all day long even though you aren't tied down to a classroom of children as they are. You'll have to work hard to avoid the perception that you have more time than they do. Post your daily, weekly, or monthly schedule on your door and let teachers know what your plans are by holding an orientation session early in the year. Teacher orientation will be discussed in detail later. Some counselors publish a monthly newsletter to communicate with staff and parents. Others choose to make brief oral presentations at faculty meetings throughout the year. Choose some avenue to keep teachers informed about upcoming guidance happenings.

Individual communication and consultation with teachers can also strengthen your relationship with them. Make it a point to be visible in the mornings before school and for a while after school so that teachers can talk with you. Go to them with follow-up information when they have referred students or requested your help.

As counselor you will often serve as a "bridge" between teachers and administrators or between teachers and parents. Your training and communication skills will help you empathize and serve as a support to teachers, parents, and administrators without choosing sides. Remember to act professionally and ethically. Be careful to avoid **Pothole #1: GOSSIP**. Teachers talk to other teachers. Parents talk to other parents and teachers. When you need to unload after a stressful meeting, and you will, find a fellow counselor or supportive administrator to confide in. Counselors need counseling too. This will be discussed further in Chapter 8.

Setting Up Your Office

Whether your "space" is a closet or an entire classroom, there are a few essentials to remember:

1) Make your office area attractive and inviting. Decorate it with colorful, age-appropriate pictures, pillows, curtains, etc. Include child-size furniture. It's alright to have an adult chair or two for parent conferences, but when meeting with children, offer them a choice of seats and adjust your level to theirs. Their choice can also give you valuable information for your counseling session. Add to the inviting climate by displaying student art work with their permission.

2) Avoid physical obstacles to open communication. If you have a desk, place it against a wall so that it does not create a barrier between you and the person you are helping.

3) Some basic items to include in your office are: telephone, computer or word processor, mirror, toy box or basket, children's books, art supplies, small table and chair, puppets, file cabinet, professional bookshelf. If you're interested in setting up an area for play therapy, a more detailed list of suggested items can be found in the appendix.

Working With A Partner or Going It Alone

I have had the experience of working solo and with several different partners. If you're in a large school, you may work with a partner. Hopefully you met the other counselor before you accepted this position. Merging two personalities and work styles is much like building a successful marriage. It takes communication, compromise, and a lot of hard work. Ideally, partners can plan together and implement a total developmental guidance program with each contributing their strengths to the program. If, however, you find yourself paired with someone very difficult to work with, or with an extremely different philosophy from your own, you can still have an effective program by dividing the work load and each "doing your own thing." It is to your advantage, however, to try to work out your differences because it is very helpful to have a partner to consult with on difficult cases or after you've had a frustrating day.

New counselors are especially vulnerable to "burnout". Warning! Beware of **Pothole #2: ISOLATION**. Don't try to handle this job all by yourself. Get some support for yourself so you can be the best you can be. Every one of us was a new counselor at some time, so no one will think less of you for asking questions. If you were a classroom teacher, you probably worked with a team or grade level group. If you are the only counselor in the school you'll need to connect with a mentor. This can be a district guidance coordinator if available, or another counselor in the district, or other special area  "one-of-a-kind" teacher such as art, music, speech, etc. The support you'll receive through this networking will help combat isolation.

Materials Mania

If you're in a new school, you'll probably be responsible for ordering materials for the guidance office. On the other hand, if your school has an established program, you may have an annual budget for adding materials each year. Some elementary schools have no allotted budget, but may find funding in the total school budget at the principal's discretion. Whatever the case, first take inventory of the materials you have and those in the school library which may be appropriate for your use. Visit other schools with established programs and look at materials first hand if possible. Sometimes catalog descriptions can be misleading and lead to wasted expenditures.

Counseling conventions and conferences are also good places to preview materials before buying. If your budget is limited, or non-existent, contact experienced counselors in your district. Most are willing to share their files and materials with you to "try before you buy". You will soon find materials that suit your personality, budget and teaching style.

Another excellent resource for ideas is PIC (Practical Ideas for Counselors), a monthly publication from Marco, that can be ordered by your school librarian for a nominal yearly fee.

Once you've researched a little, order a few things, then add a few more items each year. Keep an inventory list of materials by topic for easy reference. Believe it or not, some schools have more materials than the counselors can remember, so it helps save time later to sort and store them topically if possible. A list of suggested elementary guidance materials can be found in the appendix.

Meeting the Staff

There is one of you and dozens of them. If you are new to the school, chances are it will take you a few weeks to learn all the names of your faculty and staff. Work on it! If learning names is not your strong suit, provide name tags for the staff to wear the first few days of school. Study a school yearbook or teacher roster. Introduce yourself as often as necessary. Every staff member should know who you are and where your office/room is located.

Get to know and appreciate the school secretaries. It has been my experience that secretaries are usually overworked and grossly underpaid, so give them your respect and appreciation. Try to do your own typing, filing, etc. so as not to burden them by your presence. If you have a secretary assigned to help in guidance you are extremely fortunate; treat him/her accordingly.

Custodians and maintenance workers are other essential staff members to become acquainted with. Take the time to start their day with a cheerful "good morning", and make it a point to compliment their work when you notice a job well done. Your encouragement will pay off when you need their cooperation and assistance later.

It goes without saying that you will need to work closely with your administrator/s. Once again, effective communication is vital to a good working relationship. It takes time and effort to gain their trust. Don't burden him/her with every minor detail and decision, but be sure to keep your principal informed of pertinent transactions with students, parents, and teachers...especially if there's a problem they may have to deal with later. An administrator's nightmare is to get caught "off guard" by an angry parent. Try to diffuse tension whenever possible, but give your principal advance warning and background information if a confrontation is imminent. Want to make a good impression on your principal? Anticipate his/her needs and wishes before he/she asks. Act immediately when he/she makes referrals to you or requests information, and give prompt feedback or response. It's a great feeling to be able to respond to an administrative referral by saying, "Oh, I noticed Johnny in your office a lot lately, so I talked with him and placed him in a small group to work on peer relations." That's impressive!

Remember when I referred to the counselor's role as being in "no man's land?" You'll realize soon enough that you don't really fit in with the teachers in the same way you used to, and you may miss those team meetings and group gripe sessions. (Who'd have ever believed it?) This is where networking with other support staff becomes important. Seek out others who work alone...the nurse, special area teachers, secretary, etc., and establish a relationship with some of them. You may want to eat lunch together. This will help you avoid the pothole of "ISOLATION" while adjusting to your new role.

Information You'll Need

In my district, I work five extra days before the teachers return to school from their summer vacation. If you don't have this paid time, and even if you do, you'll probably want to put in some of your own time to get organized before school starts.

You'll need a teacher roster, master schedule, and floor plan of the school. A school calendar denoting holidays also helps with long-range planning.

Points to Remember
Chapter 1

1. When you put on the counselor's "hat," you must give up the role of "disciplinarian".
2. Avoid teachers' lounge GOSSIP.
3. Set up a "child-friendly" office.
4. Network with another counselor to avoid ISOLATION.
5. Order and familiarize yourself with materials.
6. Get to know your staff.
7. Gather information you'll need before starting to plan your schedule.

©2003 YouthLight, Inc.

FIGURE 1-1

Small Office Floor Plan

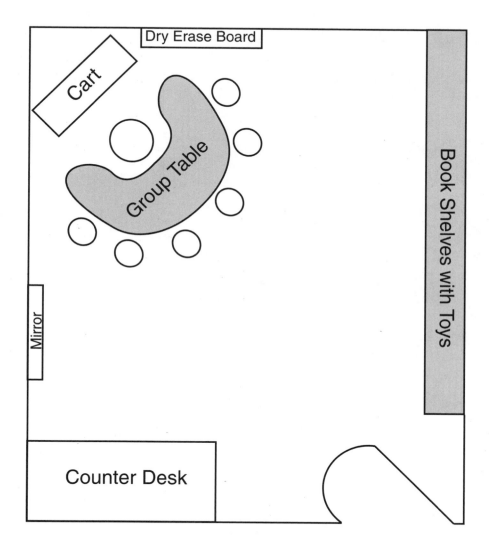

Large Office Floor Plan

```
┌──────┐
│ Sand │
│ Tray │
└──────┘
```

FIGURE 1-1 continued

Office Floor Plan
for Two Counselors

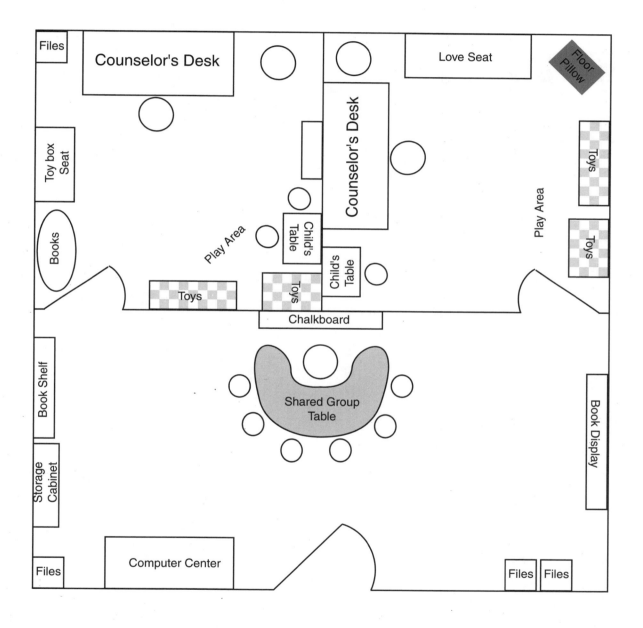

CHAPTER 2

Get Set!
(First Two Weeks of School)

What to Expect the First Day of School

One thing you can expect on the first day or two of school is the unexpected. Most administrators will assign all non-homeroom personnel to special duties to help the year get off to a smooth start. Don't panic if you are asked to cover bus duty or help out in the office with new registrants. Many parents wait until the first official day of school to register their children, so the office will likely be swamped. Pitch in and help out wherever needed. After the dust settles, you can get on with your guidance responsibilities. If you are in a primary school, there will probably be a few tears from kindergarten and first grade youngsters leaving their parent(s) or guardian(s) for the first time. You can help parents and children by greeting them warmly and offering to walk the reluctant students to class. The quicker the break from parents, the better. You may want to make a follow-up phone call to anxious parents later in the day to reassure them that Johnny or Susie is adjusting nicely. (If a child suffers from chronic separation anxiety beyond the first few days of school, you may want to share with their parents a copy of the article I have included at the end of this chapter.) Once students are in their classrooms, you'll have time to retreat to your office to work on planning your year.

People to Know

Make a special effort to meet the support personnel in your school. You will work close-ly with the school psychologist and the school nurse. Other support staff that you may make referrals to or consult with include the speech therapist, ESL (English as a sec-ond language) teacher, occupational and physical therapists, special education resource teacher, fine arts teachers, etc. Many times the counselor is the contact person for referrals to these support services. If you will be responsible for processing referrals for psychological testing, you will need to arrange a meeting early on with the psychol-ogist and principal to set up procedures. This can involve a lot of time and paperwork, so it is essential to have a plan and carry it out in a consistent, organized manner.

Setting Up Your Schedule

If you don't plan your schedule, someone else will. Watch out for **Pothole #3: UNSTRUCTURED TIME**. A counselor must be both structured and flexible. This sounds like a contradiction, but it is truly necessary. It is easy to fall into the habit of reacting to oth-ers' needs and requests rather than setting an agenda of your own. Before you know it, a day has passed and you haven't accomplished anything on your guidance program agenda. Your schedule should include structured time segments for classroom guidance lessons as well as time for unplanned emergencies. If you have a class sched-uled, you will not be free to cover unexpected non-guidance duties that may come up. I have had the good fortune of working for administrators that understand the bound-aries of the guidance and counseling role, but you will not always find that to be the case.

If there are two or more counselors, first decide which classes each will serve. The load can be divided by grade level, by location in the building, or by interest of the coun-selors. It's best to divide the student/teacher population so that you will be responsi-ble for all guidance services to that population. In other words, you are the counselor for the same children that you teach in classroom guidance. This provides the optimum situation for getting to know students and providing continuity in services. Of course, either counselor can help out in an emergency or when the other is absent. If one counselor is not available, and it is not an emergency, take a message and tell the teacher, parent, etc. that you will have the other counselor who serves that student contact them. It's better not to get into the habit of trying to "fix it" quickly and/or having to relay second-hand information to your partner.

After classrooms have been assigned to a counselor, decide how many classes you can comfortably handle in a week, allowing time for other responsibilities. For example, if I serve 25 homerooms, I may decide to schedule 7-10 classes a week for 3 consecutive weeks. Or, I may decide to schedule those classes throughout the month. Using the master schedule as reference, choose a time for each of your assigned classes. You may want to cluster the majority of classes in the middle of the week to avoid Monday and Friday holidays and staff development days. If you schedule lightly on Monday and Friday, it is easier to make up those classes when needed. (You may want to present your proposed schedule to teachers for feedback before locking it in.) This schedule allows me to visit each classroom 11 times during the school year. Some counselors get around to their classes every 2 weeks, some every month, depending on the size of the school and other program needs. I suggest somewhere between 8 and 12 lessons each year. A sample classroom guidance schedule follows. At first glance this may look like a light schedule, but remember this is only the very structured part of your schedule. Small groups, individual counseling, parent conferences, etc. will be plugged in later.

If you are serving several grade levels, I suggest doing all grade 1 lessons in the same week, grade 2 the next week, if possible. It makes for easier planning and is less confusing to have just one classroom lesson preparation at a time. In small schools, this won't be possible with only a few classes per grade, but you will have the alternate advantage of keeping things interesting and less monotonous.

Long Range Planning

Once you've planned your two, three, or four week cycle, you're ready to choose topics for classroom lessons. These should be selected based on school needs, district guidelines, state and federal laws, and your professional training. There are at least two ways to plan these topics. You may choose a monthly emphasis and create lessons at each grade level around this topic; or you may choose a topic to emphasize at each grade level and plan all their lessons for the year around this topic. I have done it both ways. Starting out, I believe the monthly topics are more workable. Two samples of yearly program outlines are included in this chapter. I try to have this ready to give to teachers at their orientation session the first week of school. In addition to these yearly and monthly schedules, you may later merge your group schedule with these and make a weekly schedule to post on your door which includes current group times, times for teacher consultation, individual counseling, etc. This, of course, will include some firm commitments and some flexible time.

Orientation

Orientation is your first opportunity to advertise your program. It should be done for three audiences: parents, faculty, and students.

Parent orientation may consist of a colorful brochure sent home with students, or it can be a part of a school-wide Meet the Teacher night. Your brochures should outline guidance services and give the counselor's name and school telephone number. Business cards are a nice "extra" to give out at registration or after a meeting with parents. Some school counselors prepare short videos or computer generated slide shows to introduce themselves to parents.

Faculty orientation to guidance should be conducted within the first week or two of school. Ask your principal to put you on the agenda for a faculty meeting. Plan to take about 15-20 minutes going over your plans, philosophy, procedures, and schedule. This is a good time to emphasize your new role as counselor not disciplinarian. Therefore, teachers are asked to remain in their classrooms during classroom guidance presentations.

This also makes it possible for them to integrate and follow-up on your lesson objectives and to give valid evaluation feedback on your end-of-the-year survey.

Provide a colorful folder for each teacher containing schedules, helpful or inspirational messages, child abuse reporting information, referral forms, community resources, and anything else you choose. Ask them to keep these handy for quick reference. I thank teachers in advance for using written referral forms. It helps me remember referral information and provides documentation which may protect both of us later. I use these forms to document my interventions with the student.

Student orientation should take place in the first 2-3 weeks of school. This can be a regular length lesson (20-40 minutes depending on grade level) or a brief introductory visit (10 minutes). The abbreviated visits will require another schedule unless teachers are flexible enough to allow you to pop in unannounced. I have done it successfully both ways.

For your student orientation, choose something visual to use as you introduce yourself and your job to the students. Presentations may include a special puppet friend, a hat, a magic trick, a bag or suitcase (counselor's bag), a poster, etc. Young children may not remember your name, but they will remember your puppet or the magic trick you did. I don't mind being remembered as "the rainbow lady," the "magic trick lady," or the "lady with the parrot puppet." The name will come with later contacts. Be sure to include in your visit, instructions for student self-referral. I have a mailbox in the hallway outside my office. Students can look for the rainbow (or whatever visual you choose) on the wall and on the mailbox where they put their note or referral form. Kindergarten children can just tell their teacher that they want to see me. Sample orientation presentations and handouts are included at the end of this chapter.

Communication with Teachers

Clear and effective communication with teachers is essential in building a strong guidance program. Communication may be oral or written. Brief written notes will suffice in some situations. In the "busyness" of your day, it is easy to fall into **Pothole #4, POOR COMMUNICATION.** If you expect teachers to make referrals to you for counseling, you must earn their respect by giving prompt and helpful feedback to them. This doesn't mean you have to tell them everything that happens in the privacy of the counseling session, but it does necessitate keeping them informed of important issues in the lives of the students you work with. When you meet with a student individually or in a small group, it is a professional courtesy to let them know within ethical boundaries why you're seeing the child, and what they can do to help support him/her. In cases of family or emotional difficulties, it may help the teacher be more sensitive to the child's needs, if he/she knows a little background information.

If the teacher is requesting help with a student's behavior, follow-up is essential! Try to gain an understanding of the goal of the child's misbehavior (Dreikers), assess the teacher's management style, then tactfully offer practical suggestions for behavior modification. Be careful to avoid sounding like a "know-it-all." Always empathize with the teacher's position in the classroom. ("It's really hard to think fast on your feet when you're busy with 20 other children.") You may want to offer ideas for motivating and reinforcing appropriate behavior at this time. Beware of **Pothole # 5, DISCIPLINE.**

Sometimes a teacher will give a child a verbal thrashing in front of you in a desperate effort to gain validation and support for his/her current feelings of frustration. Remember, it is never the counselor's job to scold, lecture, or judge a student for misbehavior. It is appropriate to help the student understand his/her feelings about personal self-defeating behaviors and support him/her in changing them if he/she so desires. Remember, you may be the only person in the school who can separate the child from the behavior and love that child as he/she is...flaws and all. That doesn't mean you condone the misbehavior, but you refuse to reject or dislike the whole child because of the behavior. If you can establish a genuine relationship with the child based on acceptance of him/her as he/she is, you will have the foundation for growth in positive behaviors.

Counselor Follow-Up to Teachers

Child's Name: _____

Class: _____

Referral Source: _____

_____

Contact Made: _____

Message: _____

_____

_____

_____

_____

_____

Forms, Forms, and More Forms

In my constant struggle to become more organized and efficient, I enjoy creating, and using a variety of artistic and helpful forms. Using clip art or your own, you can design attractive customized forms to use for teacher referrals, student self-referrals, appointment slips, group notices, etc. You may want to utilize the school mascot or a favorite picture symbol that students associate with you. (rainbow, heart, etc.) Even when sending out memos to staff members, using "eye-catching" visuals increases the chances of the memo being read before ending up in "file 13."

This is an area that is subject to personal preferences, but I have included a few of my favorite ones—parent letters and permissions referral forms (student and teacher), appointment slips, group notices, group summaries, (see figures on pages 33 - 44). Feel free to choose and use the ones you like—-incorporating your school mascot, symbol, colors or your favorite pictures to personalize them.

Points to Remember
Chapter 2

1. Expect the unexpected on the first day of school.
2. Get to know support staff.
3. Plan your work; work your plan. Avoid too much UNSTRUCTURED TIME. If you don't schedule your time, someone else will.
4. Conduct guidance orientation for all audiences.
5. Maintain good COMMUNICATION with teachers.
6. The counselor should not DISCIPLINE students.
7. Use forms to help you become organized and efficient.

FIGURE 2-1

Sample September

Classroom Guidance Schedule

Sunday	Monday	Tuesday	Wednesday	Thursday	Friday	Saturday
			1 9:40-10:10 4D Rhodes 12:30-1:00 4A Hall	2 9:40-10:10 4E Metzger 12:30-1:00 4B Hinson	3 9:40-10:10 4C Helmrich	4
5	6 1:00-1:30 2G Terry	7 9:45-10:15 2A Guess 12:30-1:00 2E Weathers	8 9:45-10:15 2B Fitchett 1:00-1:30 2F Priam	9 9:45-10:15 2C Mercer 1:10-1:40 2D Theobald	10	11
12	13	14 10:30-11:00 5D Hartnett 12:30-1:00 5A Sage	15 10:30-11:00 5E Rasado 1:10-1:40 5B Farmer	16 10:30-11:00 5F Davis 1:10-1:40 5C McKevlin	17	18
19	20	21 9:40-10:10 4D Rhodes 12:30-1:00 4A Hall	22 9:40-10:10 4E Metzger 12:30-1:00 4B Hinson	23 9:40-10:10 4C Helmrich	24	25
26	27 1:00-1:30 2G Terry	28 9:45-10:15 2A Guess 12:30-1:00 2E Weathers	29 9:45-10:15 2B Fitchett 1:00-1:30 2F Priam	30 9:45-10:15 2C Mercer 1:10-1:40 2D Theobald	Because the counselor should not be a disciplinarian, we ask that teachers remain with classes during classroom guidance lessons. Thanks!	

FIGURE 2-2

Sample Small Group Counseling Schedule

Times	Monday	Tuesday	Wednesday	Thursday	Friday
8:00-8:30					New "Bees"
8:30-9:00		Families in Transition			
9:00-9:30				Anger Management	
9:30-10:00					
10:00-10:30					
10:30-11:00	Self-Esteem				
11:00-11:30					
11:30-12:00					
12:00-12:30					
12:30-1:00	Divorce		Peer Relations		
1:00-1:30					Family Illness
1:30-2:00		Families in Transition	Anger Management		

Coming Attractions!

Guidance Emphases for the Year

Aug. 26-Sept. 20 Orientation to Guidance

Sept. 23-Dec. 17 Conflict Management
(Classes will be scheduled for 5
consecutive weekly lessons)

January	Responsibility/Study Skills
February	Individual Differences
March	Substance Awareness
April	Career Awareness
May	Safety

Special Events:

October	Red Ribbon Week
January	Personal Safety Curriculum
February	Nation School Counseling Week
	Warm Fuzzy Week
May	Substance Prevention Club
	Last Blast

McGruff's Pals: Substance Prevention
Club for second graders will be
scheduled throughout the year.

FIGURE 2-4

Guidance Program
"Year-At-A-Glance"

Theme: "Guidance Helps People Grow to "Bee" Their Best"

Emphases for the year will be:

PD/CD/K ....Self-Awareness and Language/Feelings Expression

1st Grade...............................Appropriate School Behavior ("Beehive Behavior")

2nd Grade ....Interpersonal Relations/Positive Peer Relations

3rd Grade ....Responsible Work Habits/Study Skills

4th Grade ....Making Responsible Decisions

5th Grade ....Career Awareness/Personal Growth & Change

We will also review conflict management and teach substance awareness at all levels. We will focus on integrating the 12 National Career Competencies into classroom lessons and encourage you to do the same.

Teachers are encouraged to reinforce and integrate classroom guidance topics into your curriculum. Let us know if your class has special needs that we can address or help you address through materials we may have.

Classes will be scheduled on a three-week cycle (except during spring testing weeks). We will provide you with a monthly calendar as well as weekly reminders just prior to our visits. We appreciate your presence during our presentations to continue your regular discipline plan and to observe and give us feedback.

Special Events: Red Ribbon Week - October
Personal Safety Unit - January - February
"Bee Buddies" for new students, and others to be announced.

TEACHER ORIENTATION TO GUIDANCE SERVICES

ACTIVITY

MATERIALS: Small Styrofoam cup, knitting needle, pitcher of water, Aqua Slush (a powdery substance which when added to a liquid turns it into a thick slush.). Handout...Under the Guidance Umbrella or other handout of your choice; prepared teacher folders including sample referral forms, other helpful information. (If you don't have time to prepare folders by the first few days of school, you can deliver them to teachers as you visit classrooms to orient students.)

PROCEDURE: I'm going to try to impress you with a magic trick. As we go along, will you let me know when you're impressed? I'm going to try to make water disappear.

First, I'll pour some water in this cup. (Cup will look empty, but will have some aqua slush in the bottom of it.) Are you impressed yet?

Now I will poke this knitting needle through the cup without spilling any water. (Poke needle all the way through the cup and out other side.) Are you impressed?

OK, this will really impress you! Abracadabra! (Turn cup upside down holding onto needle.)Are you impressed? Great! I've been practicing all summer for this.

Now, what does this trick have to do with our guidance program? Well, a couple of thoughts about that. First, things are not always what they seem. Just as there seemed to be water in this cup, sometimes we have illusions about the children and families we teach. A child may appear to be from a perfect family while he or she may have hidden problems or concerns. On the other hand, we may judge a child from an obviously dysfunctional family as a child with problems, when he or she may be coping very well. Similarly, in the guidance office or program, things are not always what they seem to be. Keep that in mind and remember to look beyond the obvious. Please ask us if you have questions or concerns.

Secondly, don't expect to be impressed by what we do with children! We don't claim to be able to work magic with every child....and certainly not instantly. I wish we could, but we all know that problems take time to develop and time to be resolved...and environment bears a heavy influence. So let's be patient with each other, and hopefully we can realize some small victories for our children. Some of our work may not bear fruit until weeks or even years have passed.

We want to take a few minutes now to respond to the needs revealed through our survey last spring, and to orient you to our district and school program. Our district has a Comprehensive Guidance Program. We don't just do whatever we want to, but we plan our school program within the boundaries and guidelines of the district and state framework.

Handout: "Under the Guidance Umbrella" Go over the four components.

1) **Curriculum**: structured teaching experiences that provide information to students and parents.

2) **Individual Planning**: Not counselor planning...student planning. These are activities to help students manage their personal growth in relationships, educational development, career education. (examples: placement input, consultation, study skills helps).

3) **Responsive Services**: This is the largest chunk of our time. Last year we saw over 400 individual students and some 200 in small groups. Some of you requested more small groups...perhaps because students in your class did not attend. We ran from 5-8 groups each a week, which is about the maximum we can handle effectively. Let us know if your students have special needs and we will do our best to prioritize them and get them into groups.

4) **System Support**: These are activities which promote and enhance the total school program. This piece of the program is getting larger every year.

Explain referral procedures, child abuse reporting law and procedures, overview of your yearly plans, School-to-Work Transition Act of 1994 (SC), etc.

School-to-Work: Some of you wonder why we do career awareness activities in the primary grades. The law in SC states that schools will provide a comprehensive career awareness curriculum in grades K-12. It is the law...and it is just a good idea to make learning relevant to students of any age. Career awareness at the elementary level is the responsibility of all school staff.

We'll be conducting more extensive staff development later in regard to this law.

Remember that we are here to support you and your students in any way we can. Please call on us and come by and check out the resources that we have available for your use.

ACTIVITY

STUDENT ORIENTATION TO GUIDANCE

(K-3rd/10 minutes)

Hello boys and girls! I'm _____ and this is my friend, Amos (or whatever you name your puppet). Say hello to the boys and girls, Amos. (Amos hides his face shyly.) That's all right, Amos. I know it's a little scary meting a whole room full of strangers. How many of you felt a little shy or nervous your first day of school? Let's make Amos feel better by introducing ourselves to him. How about saying one of your favorite foods in front of your name. (Amos whispers to me.) Oh, he says he's "Applesauce Amos." (Amos is a monkey puppet. He never says anything aloud to class, but whispers in my ear. This is a good way to start out if you're shy, as I was, about doing puppetry.) I'm "Banana Bender." (Proceed around classroom giving each student a turn. Allow passing if a child is too shy, or can't think of a food.)

Thank you. I hope we can all be friends. (Amos whispers again.) Amos wants to know why he's the only monkey in this class. I think that's another reason he's so shy. It's hard sometimes being new or different. Are any of you new to _____ (school) this year? WELCOME! I'm really glad you came to _____ (school). Amos, just because you're different, that doesn't keep us from being friends. Right boys and girls? (Right!) Besides, we're all different in some ways and we all feel scared, shy, lonely, sad, or worried sometimes. In fact, that's why I'm here. As your guidance counselor, part of my job is to talk with students when they feel scared, shy, confused, lonely, angry, sad, or worried. A counselor is someone who listens to almost anything you have to say and tries to help if you have a problem. (Amos whispers.) Amos wants to know if he can tell me a secret. Yes, Amos, you can tell me a problem that is a secret and I'll keep your secret unless it's a secret that might cause you to get hurt. Then I would have to tell someone who could keep you safe. (Amos whispers.) Amos wants to know what else a counselor does? Does anyone know? (Allow students to answer.) I'll also come to your class every 3 weeks to share a learning activity with you. I will give your teacher, _____, these forms for you to fill out and put in my mail box when you have a problem that you can't work out on your own. Who can tell Amos what my mailbox looks like? (Describe mailbox...it has a rainbow on it, etc.) When I get your note, I will make an appointment to meet with you in the next day or two. I'll come to your class to get you. We'll work together to help you feel better.

Some of you may come to see me in a small group with other students to learn about things like divorce, making friends, or doing better in school.

But, even if you never need my help with a problem, I'll still get to know you when I visit your classroom.

Are there any questions?

I have a note for you to take home to your parents for me. It tells them what I do here at school. They may call me if they need to. (Discuss times a parent might call and ask the counselor to see his/her child.) I hope I'll get to meet your parents this year at PTA meetings or parent workshops that we will have.

Have a great year in _____grade! Come on Amos. It's time to visit another class and meet some more new friends. (Amos whispers.) Amos wants to thank you for being so nice to him. BYE! BYE! (wave Amos' hand)

ACTIVITY

ORIENTATION and GUIDANCE LESSON

(2nd-5th/ 30 minutes)

LESSON: What's in the Bag? (orientation and self-awareness lesson)

MATERIALS: My gym bag is full of personal items of interest to me such as musical tapes, gym shoes, gardening tool, etc., a gift bag containing cards stating the duties of the school counselor, half-sheet of drawing paper for each student, one copy of worksheet for Activity 4 from Learning to Care, 1983 Scott Foresman and Company.

PROCEDURE: Introduce yourself to students and welcome them to the school. Show them your two bags and ask them if anyone can guess what's inside the gym bag first. Then the gift bag. Say: "Things are not always what they seem. We all have different ideas and look at things differently because we are all unique. We'll look inside the bags in a minute, but first I want you to stretch your brains a little. Show worksheet picture of vase/faces. What do you see? Discuss different points of view emphasizing that sometimes two people can look at the same thing and see something different Now, let's go back to my bags.

This is my Counselor's Bag. Have students take turns pulling out a card and reading it. Briefly explain each duty. Hand out the "Make Tracks to Guidance" sheet or your own orientation handout and go over it. Be sure students understand the self-referral process, mail box, etc. Answer questions.

This is my personal bag. Now dump out contents of gym bag and share a few of the contents and what each tells about your personal interests. Answer questions/discuss.

Say: "Now you know a little about me. I would like to know something about each of you. Let's brainstorm for a few seconds...stretch your brains to name as many different kinds of bags as you can think of." (gym, trash, shopping, golf, teacher, book, suitcase, briefcase, lunch, etc.) Ask students to draw their own bags and contents that tell us something about them. Have volunteers share as time allows.

Hand out parent brochures and ask students to deliver. Close by letting students know when you'll be back to see them.

STUDENT ORIENTATION TO GUIDANCE

(feelings, K-3)

ACTIVITY

MATERIALS: Feelings Street Signs placed around room (Enlarge feelings faces and label with names below), magic cylinder (directions to make will follow)

SCRIPT: "Hello boys and girls! I'm _____ and I'm your counselor or grown-up friend here at _____Elementary. Raise your hand if you like to play games. Well, good, because we're going to play some games today to help us get to know each other.

What's my name again?

OK. The first game we'll play is called '1,2,3, Put a Feeling On Your Face.'
Can you say that with me? (Have students practice saying it aloud.) "1,2,3, Put a feeling on your face."

Very good. Now, I'm going to turn my back to you and put a feeling on my face. I want you to say when I hold up my fingers, '1,2,3, put a feeling on your face.' Then I'll turn around and show you a feeling. You can guess what that feeling is."

After a few feelings faces (happy, sad, angry, scared) tell the children that we are going on a make-believe bus ride to the "Land of Feelings." Have everyone stand up and follow you in a line. Remind students to be very quiet on the bus so we'll have a safe trip and so we can hear what the driver says. "I'm the driver. OK, let's go."

Slowly lead class around room to "Feelings Bus Stop Signs." At each stop ask students how many have felt that feeling. Briefly let one or two students tell about each feeling. Signs I used were: **Happy Haven, Sad State, Angry Avenue** and **Scared Street.** Pretend to get "back to school" and have students return to their seats. Ask students which place in the "Land of Feelings" they like to visit.

"Sit down and I'll show you another game. Do you like magic tricks?
I have a special magic cylinder. I'll use this to show you how I try to help boys and girls. Sometimes boys and girls have 'yucky' feelings, kind of like a fowl smelling fish." (Open up one end of the cylinder and pour out paper 'fishy feelings.') Read out the names of feelings written on fish—-sad, scared, etc. These feelings are not bad, but they can make us feel yucky sometimes. "Do you ever want to get rid of yucky old

fishy feelings? OK. Let's put them back in the magic cylinder. Does anyone know a magic word?" (Get one from student and all say it together.) Turn the fishy feelings into sweet smelling flowers. (Pour paper cut-out flowers out of other end of cylinder and read feelings words...happy, love, etc.)

Explain to students that coming to guidance—-my room—-is kind of like this trick. "You may come in feeling yucky and we'll talk and play together and try to help you feel happy again.

I'll also come visit you here in your classroom once a month. Some of you will come to my room by yourself or in small groups."

Explain referral process. Give handouts for students and parents.

Directions for Magic Cylinder:
Glue or tape together bottom to bottom, two plastic cylinder containers. Cover with contact paper so they look like one long cylinder. There should be a screw-off lid on each end of cylinder. Discreetly mark one end so you'll know where the fish are. When the class is saying the magic word, move cylinder around in the air so that you will open the other end when it's time for the flowers to appear.

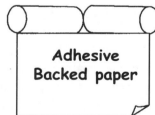

ACTIVITY

STUDENT ORIENTATION TO GUIDANCE SERVICES

(2nd - 5th)

MATERIALS: flashlight, miniature lighthouse, or magic light bulb, handout for students appropriate to their level

Counselor introduces him/herself. Recognizes new students to the school and has them introduce themselves and tell where they came from.

Show object (flashlight, etc.) and ask what it is used for. Say: "How many of you have been in the dark when the electricity went off? How did you feel at first? What made you feel better?

Think of some other kinds of light and what they do for us. Sun, lighthouse, light bulbs, fire, etc. Just like the flashlight helps us find our way in the dark, as your counselor, I want to help guide you when you feel scared, worried or confused or 'in the dark' about something.

Think of me as your flashlight (lighthouse, etc.) that helps you find your way, like a lighthouse helps a ship find its way to the shore."

Show students self-referral forms and explain the process for referring to guidance.

Mention monthly visits to classroom.

Allow questions about guidance program...what counselor's do.

Hand out color sheet, bookmark, etc. and parent brochures.

SCHOOL COUNSELORS HELP STUDENTS SAIL TOWARDS SUCCESS!

YOUR COUNSELOR IS _____

Counselors Help Children Sail
Toward Success!

Your counselor this year is _____

FIGURE 2-5

Sample Parent Letter

Dear Parent(s)/Guardian(s):

I am your child's school counselor. Did you know that elementary counselors...
   ...teach classroom guidance lessons on a variety of topics?
   ...counsel individual students as needed and maintain confidentiality?
   ...counsel with small groups of children with similar concerns?
   ...consult with teachers and assist them in meeting individual student needs?
   ...coordinate referrals to school and community agencies?
   ...coordinate state testing programs?
   ...maintain an information center in the Guidance Office for parent and
      teacher use?

Guidance services are available to all parent(s)/guardian(s) and their children.
Please feel free to call me if you have a concern or a question. I am looking forward to meeting you.

FIGURE 2-6

Sample Student Letter

Hello Boys and Girls!

I am your school counselor. A counselor is someone who can help you when you feel worried, sad, confused, angry, or lonely. In my room you can:

    ...talk about things that are important to you.
    ...play games to help you learn about yourself and others.
    ...talk with other children.
    ...just sit and think.

Follow the rainbow to find my room.

Your friend,

FIGURE 2-7

Make Tracks to Guidance When...

...you feel worried, sad, scared, angry or lonely and want to talk about your feelings.

...you need help with problem-solving.

...you want help coping with changes in your family.

Your school counselor this year is _____.

FIGURE 2-8

Hello Busy Bees!
I'm "hoppy" to "bee"
your counselor.

Mrs. Bender

"Buzz" on down to guidance
when you need......
.....to talk about your feelings.
.....time-out to sit and think.
.....help with problem-solving.
.....to share important news.

Elementary Guidance

GUIDANCE COUNSELORS • SCHOOL • ARE THE HEART OF THE SCHOOL

Dorchester School District Two

Please contact your child's counselor if you have any concerns about your child including:

* Classroom performance

* Family changes (moving, death, divorce, or separation)

* Home stress

* Interpretation of standardized test results

* Parenting

* Classroom behavior

* Sudden change in child's behavior

* Peer relations

* Responsibility

Your child's counselor is:

Used with permission from Dorchester County Schools District Two

FIGURE 2-10

Topics Taught During Classroom Guidance Include -

- Individual differences
- peer relations
- substance abuse awareness and prevention
- career awareness
- study skills
- decision making
- self-esteem
- safety

In Individual and/or group counseling we...

...help children cope with difficult and/or unchangeable life events.

...help children recognize and make use of their potential.

...give children the opportunity to share their feelings and concerns.

...develop problem-solving ability.

...teach decision making skills.

...build self-esteem and confidence.

The Elementary School Guidance Counselor

Counsels individually with children

Teaches monthly guidance lessons in classrooms

Conducts small group counseling sessions

Processes referrals for the testing of special needs children

Consults with parents in private conferences about their child

Consults with teachers

Conducts parenting workshops

Participates in curriculum development

Provides information on community resources for families

Used with permission from Dorchester County Schools District Two

Under the Guidance Umbrella

The school counselor is a counselor, facilitator, coordinator, and consultant.

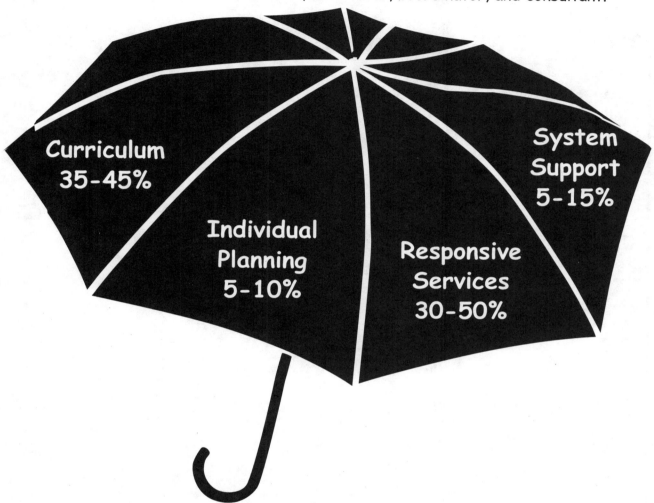

CURRICULUM	INDIVIDUAL PLANNING	RESPONSIVE SERVICES	Crisis Intervention
Classroom Guidance	Placement Input	Individual Counseling	
Small Group Guidance	Consultation	Small Group Counseling	
Parent Education	Individual Assessment		
Substance Awareness	Individual Advisement	Consultation	
Career Development		Referral	

Credit: Missouri comprehensive guidance: A model for program development, implementation and evaluation

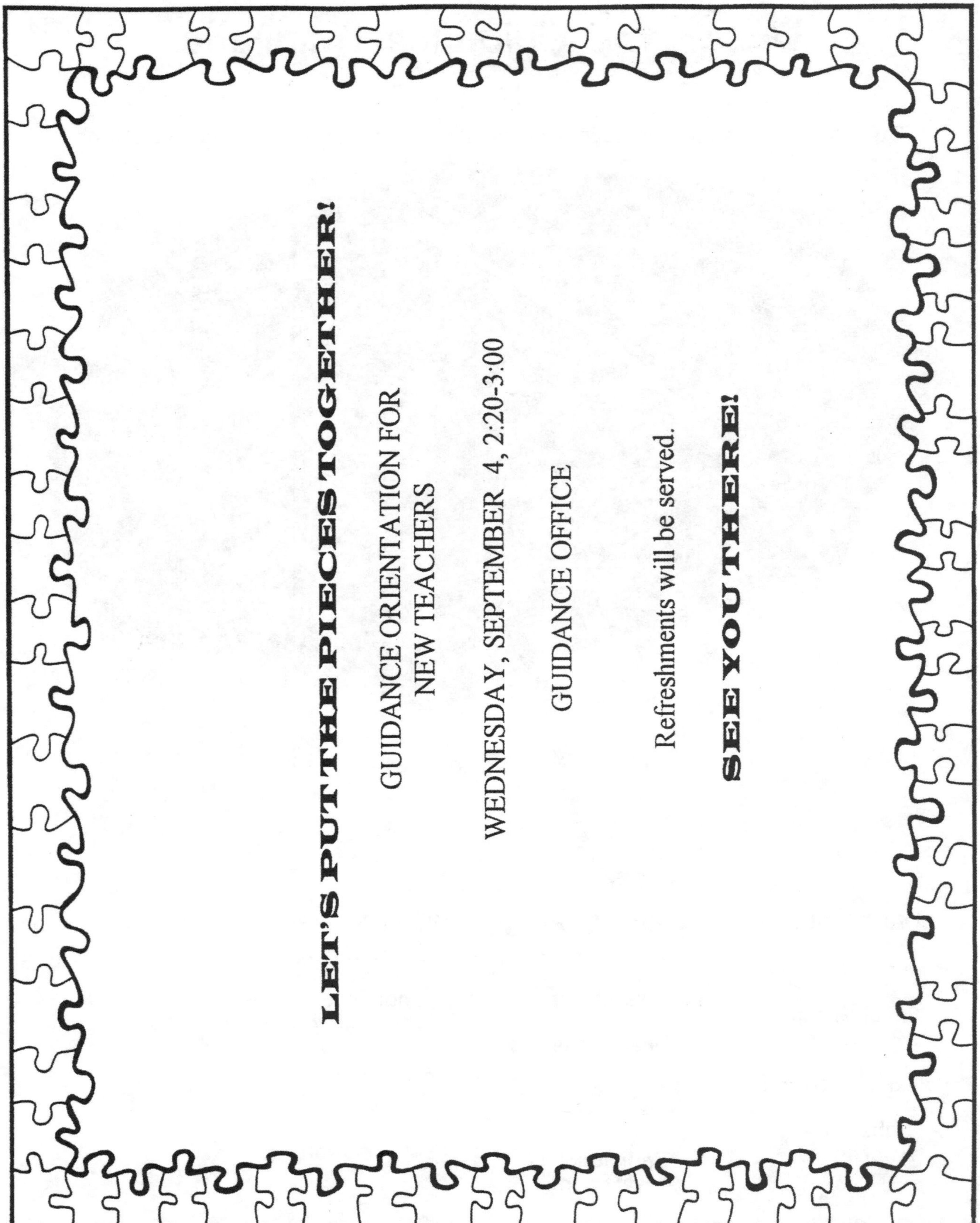

LET'S PUT THE PIECES TOGETHER!

GUIDANCE ORIENTATION FOR
NEW TEACHERS

WEDNESDAY, SEPTEMBER 4, 2:20-3:00

GUIDANCE OFFICE

Refreshments will be served.

SEE YOU THERE!

FIGURE 2-13

A Pat on the Back for You!

We all need and deserve a "pat on the back" at times. This is my "pat" for you. Why not display it on a wall in your classroom and use it as needed for yourself and your students?

Tell students to give themselves a "pat on the back" as a reward for helpful behavior. Give yourself a "pat on the back" by leaning against the hand on the wall and giving yourself a compliment. An actual pat works well too!

This exercise with the visual reminder will encourage positive interaction and mutual appreciation among classmates.

Cut out a colorful handprint to attach to this memo.

FIGURE 2-14

When to Make a Guidance Referral

Please contact your counselor and/or refer a child if...

...you suspect child abuse or neglect.

...you notice a severe change in the child's behavior.

...the child is having a difficult time dealing with family changes.

...the child's self-concept is low.

...an illness or death in the family is upsetting the child.

...you suspect extreme financial hardship in the home and the child needs supplies, shoes, etc.

...a behavior modification plan needs to be drawn up between the teacher, counselor, and child.

...the child is dwelling in a home in which there is violence, substance abuse, addiction, or recovery from these.

...the child daydreams or seems preoccupied a major portion of the day.

...the child's grades are declining.

...a child has been absent excessively.

...the child seems to concentrate on his/her home-life to the point that it interferes with school performance.

...something seems to be bothering the child.

Yellow referral forms are available outside both guidance offices and in your teacher folder.

I Need to See the Counselor

Name: _____

Class: _____

Date: _____

I Need to See the Counselor

Name: _____

Class: _____

Date: _____

FIGURE 2-16

Make a Beeline to Guidance!

*Student:*_____

*Homeroom:*_____

*Date:*_____ *Time:*_____

Thanks!

_____

I'll Be Buzzing By For Classroom Guidance

Time:_____
Date:_____
Teacher:_____

See You Then!

FIGURE 2-17

Separation Anxiety

Separation anxiety is the distress that children experience when their parents temporarily leave them. Insecurity is the main reason for separation anxiety. Children may be afraid that they will not survive if their parents are not close by to take care of them. Separation anxiety normally begins when children are between six and eight months old. It peaks in the middle of the second year, and begins to decline gradually until it ceases at approximately three years of age.

Separation anxiety may reoccur suddenly at any age in response to environmental changes and stressors. A child who has attended and enjoyed school for several years may suddenly become ill in order to stay home, or may resist getting on the bus for school. The usual complaint is "I don't want to go to school." Thus, the term "school phobia" is applied. The term "school phobia" is misleading. Clinical studies show that these kids are usually not afraid of teachers or the school building itself. They're terribly frightened to leave home.

Children may mistakenly believe that parents need their protection. School phobia often is not an evasive maneuver. Instead it can stem from a child's misdirected feeling that his or her presence at home is necessary for parents' emotional support or physical well-being. In many instances moving to a new neighborhood, death or illness of a relative, divorce, marital discord or other family changes can stimulate separation anxiety. Overprotective or fearful parents may unknowingly cause or intensify the situation.

Early warning signs of separation anxiety may be a child's reluctance to visit friends or play outside alone. Parents may want to contact the child's school counselor to help assess the severity of the situation. The counselor can help by investigating to rule out or deal with any potential sources of anxiety at school.

Firmness and calm insistence that the child attend school may help minor "school phobics." Parents can help by establishing a consistent daily routine so that the child is sure of the details of who will be there for him, when they will arrive, and where they will be if he needs them. Actions that reassure the child of the safety and security of the family may help.

In some cases, separation anxiety can be a biochemical reaction. these cases can be successfully treated by a physician with medication. Other severe cases may require psychotherapy to deal with the underlying fears.

WHEN IT'S NOT SEPARATION ANXIETY:

Sometimes a resistant child may appear to have a problem with separation anxiety when actually he/she is testing limits or trying to get his/her own way by creating an emotional situation. This is a control issue, not separation anxiety. A counselor can help assess the situation and offer assistance in implementing a discipline plan that may relieve both parent and child of the emotional power struggle.

Adapted and condensed from several sources.

CHAPTER 3

Go!
(3rd Week and Beyond)

Record Keeping/Documentation

Obviously, there is not just one way to do record-keeping, but it is important to have a system that you use consistently. Paperwork may seem like a waste of time, but the day will come when you will be glad to have that documentation. In dealing with hundreds of students, parents, and teachers, details and dates can become overwhelming. I must also confess that my memory after 18 years of counseling is not as reliable as it used to be. Sooner or later, you will receive a subpoena to family court or be asked by a social worker to verify certain information or interventions with a student. Beware of **Pothole #6, NO DOCUMENTATION.**

A child's welfare may depend on your professional record-keeping and accountability. For these reasons, I have chosen several record-keeping methods that work for me. The length of time you choose to save these records is up to you. For individual counseling, I use a large (3-inch) loose leaf notebook with alphabetical dividers. I keep a referral form on every student I see individually. Each contact is dated with a few notes about pertinent facts and my own impressions. Dates and facts about parent calls and/or conferences in regard to this student are also noted. After the referral form is full of entries, I insert a piece of ruled notebook paper to use for additional recording of session notes. These notes are for my personal use only, and are never made a part of school records. Other things kept in this notebook include release forms, notes from parents and teachers, and occasionally a student work sample such as a family drawing or letter from the student.

For small group documentation, I keep another notebook divided into group topics. In this notebook, I keep lesson plans and activities used in small groups. Pocket dividers are helpful for storing contents that are not three-hole-punched. After a group has been completed, I file the Group Summary sheets and parent permission forms in a file labeled "Groups Completed 1999", etc. If time permits, I write up a short summary of interactions during group, but this is not a necessity. I find it very hard to remember details at the end of a day, but I may note the general movement of group or outstanding progress or resistance of individuals within the group.

Another notebook I use is for storing classroom guidance lessons. I organize this notebook by topics... self-concept, responsibility, conflict management, study skills, decision-making, social skills, stress management, peer relations, etc. (I learned this tip from a first year counselor.) For the first few years, I prepared classroom lessons, used them, filed them away, and pretty much lost track of what I taught from year to year. The notebook allows me a quick reference on a given topic including the appropriate grade level and year used. I try to type up lessons in the format shown in the chapter on classroom guidance, but even hand-written plans are helpful.

While we're on the topic of record-keeping, I will share another idea that I have found fun and helpful. Think about keeping a scrapbook of your guidance program. Take pictures of your room, your bulletin boards, speakers you arrange, school-wide programs, plays or performances, parenting workshops, newspaper clippings about guidance activities, classroom guidance activities, etc. At the end of the year (or a few years) organize pictures and display attractively in a scrapbook. When I applied for my current job in this district, I took my scrapbook with me to my interview with the personnel director. She only asked me one question: Tell me about your guidance program. I handed her my scrapbook and she looked through it as we chatted. "A picture is worth a thousand words."

Legal/Ethical Issues

The best advice I can give in this area, is to join your professional organizations and utilize their workshops and materials on legal and ethical codes of behavior. The American Counseling Association provides information on ethical standards for counselors. They can also help you access affordable group liability insurance. You can find out more by writing to this address:

American Counseling Association
Insurance Trust
5999 Stevenson Avenue
Alexandria, VA 22304-3300
(800)-347-6647

Professional Organizations

Even if money is scarce, it is advisable to join your local, state and national professional organizations for counselors. Many counselor evaluation instruments include an expectation for professional affiliation and participation. I have found this to be a benefit in several ways. Memberships usually include a subscription to journals which can keep you abreast of the latest research in the counseling field. I enjoy reading about practical ideas that can be used in my school situation.

Another benefit of professional affiliation is the opportunity to attend workshops, conferences, and conventions on the state and national level. Through the years, I have gained valuable exposure to new ideas, programs, and knowledgeable speakers by attending these events. A fringe benefit is the renewed enthusiasm and stress relief that results from meeting and networking with other counselors.

Getting Student Referrals

Now that your office is set up, your classroom schedule is arranged, you're into orientation sessions, and you're getting to know the staff, how do you get started with counseling individual students? Don't worry, you'll soon have more referrals than you have time to handle. But, your first few individuals may be discovered as you conduct classroom guidance orientation sessions. Getting to know students in a large group will open up topics that need further attention individually. For example, if you do a feelings-related activity with the entire class, you may learn that one student feels sad because his/her parents have recently separated. This is an appropriate opportunity to ask, "Would you like to get together later to talk more in private?" If the student responds positively, show him/her how to fill out a self-referral form that you've just introduced to the class. Children and parents suffering from separation anxiety may be some of your earliest referrals also. You will need to keep your sixth sense "tuned in" to needs and feelings of students, parents and teachers. Once students with needs are identified, prioritize in order of urgency, and then schedule appropriate appointment times.

I have found it helpful to use a weekly appointment book divided into 15-minute time increments. I can see the whole week at a glance as I write in scheduled classroom guidance times, parent conferences, individual appointments, and later, group times. At first, your calendar won't look full, but as things get busier, it will help you stay organized and remember commitments made. It also serves as a record to refer back to, if needed, for accountability. As discussed earlier, documentation is a very important part of an effective guidance program.

As you gradually meet individual students, you will probably want to keep a log of students who are potential small group participants. I keep a pocket folder for "Groups Forming" in which I place notes about individual referrals who may be good candidates for a future small group. It may take several weeks into the school year to become aware of several students dealing with similar issues. See those individuals weekly until you have a sufficient number (3-6) to form a group. Consider personalities and behaviors of students when placing them in a group.

In setting up groups, beware of **Pothole #7: OVERLOAD**! Start with one group, then add another and another as referrals become evident. It's all right if your first groups begin in October. I try to run 4-6 groups a week for about 8 weeks, then conclude those and start another cycle after Christmas break. I have had as many as 10 groups going at a time, but that was very stressful and demanding. New counselors should limit themselves to 2 or 3 groups the first time around. As you establish lesson plans for groups and learn to manage your time, you will be able to handle more. It is better to do 2 well-planned, effective groups, than several "thrown together" ones. Enthusiasm is wonderful, but it can get you in "over your head," and you'll feel like you're running in circles trying to keep one step ahead of the next group. If you do this, you won't provide quality counseling to your students. Group logistics will be addressed later.

Support for Staff

Teaching is one of the most difficult and stressful careers I know of. I have great respect for the men and women who work on the "front lines" with our youngsters every day. Having been there myself for 10 years prior to moving into the counselor's office, I always try to remember what it was like, so that I can provide both practical and emotional support for my teachers. (If you have not been a classroom teacher, be very careful about giving advice.) Empathy and a listening ear can form a foundation of trust on which to build a positive working relationship with the teachers you serve. This doesn't happen overnight. Give it time and effort. The investment will pay off for you and the teachers. After nearly seven years in my current school, I was rewarded for this attention to staff support by the comment from a veteran teacher, "You always have good, practical ideas. Thanks!"

Sometimes, in an effort to put children first, district and school administrators may overlook the needs of the teachers. As the counselor, you must try to recognize and tactfully speak up in support of these needs without offending or alienating your administrators. I have been fortunate to work with principals who appreciate and listen to this input. Most realize that high staff morale and an overall positive school climate is vital to achieving the academic success they desire. Again, this kind of trust develops over time with consistently dependable job performance.

How do you support staff besides listening and offering ideas? Beyond the relationship of trust, you can provide workshops, support groups, and teacher in-service as needed. Teacher in-service will be addressed in the next section. I have offered support groups for teachers in assertiveness training, stress management, and communication skills. You can plan these yourself, or arrange for an outside provider to conduct them. I like to work with teachers myself to get to know them better and to stretch my own professional skills by preparing and facilitating new groups. Many times I have adapted materials that I have acquired through conventions or workshops I have attended.

Building a Relationship Bridge to Teachers

- Listen! Listen! Listen!
- Give prompt feedback to teachers when they refer students.
- Share inspirational quotations in mailboxes and prominent places.
- Be visible. Go out of your office to visit teachers throughout the school.
- Remember birthdays with a card, balloon, or note with candy attached.
- Survey teacher needs and plan your program to address these needs.
- SMILE!
- Keep busy. Never give the impression that you have time to loaf.
- Communicate guidance happenings through memos and announcements.
- Treat teachers to a drop-in during National School Counseling Week.
- Place a basket of goodies in the lounge occasionally with a note from guidance.
- Write "Warm Fuzzy" notes to teachers when you notice something worthy of a compliment.
- Show support and concern for teachers experiencing personal crises and problems.
- Offer materials and resources for teacher use on topics of need or interest.
- Participate in school social events and mingle with teachers.
- Lead a teacher support group. (stress management, new teachers, etc.)
- Attend grade level meetings and ask how you can support teachers.
- Maintain a counseling bulletin board and change regularly.
- Make appearances on student TV or radio programs.
- Offer to conduct in-service training and workshops for teachers.
- Let teachers know you will be available to assist and support them with parent conferences.
- Take time to provide a "Pat on the Back" for teachers.
- Make "good morning" rounds to your classrooms just to touch base with students and teachers.
- Show you care.
- Consider publishing a guidance newsletter.
- Be positive!
- Write thank you notes often.
- Encourage teachers to take care of themselves.

Teacher In-services

The amount of teacher in-service you provide will depend largely on your principal. It is your responsibility to let him/her know what knowledge and resources you have to offer, then let him/her decide when, and how often to utilize your services.

Most schools will require teacher training on child abuse reporting procedures and standardized testing. Beyond those, it will vary from school to school and district to district. Other possible areas for training might be: conflict management, discipline, school-to-work implementation, conducting parent conferences. These should be determined by the needs in your school.

Keep teacher in-service presentations as brief as possible and make them as exciting and interesting as possible. You may need to call on icebreakers, magic tricks, visual aides, funny stories or jokes, or "hands-on" experiences to make powerful presentations. One resource for icebreaker activities that I use is Energizers and Icebreakers by Elizabeth S. Foster.

In addition to training for the entire faculty, you may want to offer from time to time, optional teacher support groups on topics of interest such as stress management or classroom management strategies.

Public Relations

Public relations is a huge part of having a successful guidance and counseling program. It is an ongoing view of you and your program as seen through the eyes of others. The total picture consists of doing a good job and letting others know what you do. There are many sources of wise advice on maintaining positive public relations. Your national, state, and local professional organizations can provide literature on public relations. My own personal philosophy can be summed up with these five points:

1) Plan
2) Advertise
3) Work Hard
4) Build Trust
5) Evaluate

PLAN: Reading this book is a good start in planning. Eagerness and enthusiasm is no substitute for good planning. Look before you leap. Plan your work. Work your plan.

ADVERTISE: Just as in the business world, a good program or product needs to be advertised. Don't be shy about "tooting your own horn." Publicize guidance programs and events through school newsletters, flyers, etc. Give consumers (parents, school board, citizens) a road map of coming events and make sure they know who you are and what you can do for them. Many districts send home a brochure outlining the district guidance program. Other counselors send home personalized form letters or notices to introduce themselves and their program to parents. Utilize every opportunity to educate the public about your program. Volunteer to speak to Business Partners, at PTA Meetings, School Improvement Councils, civic clubs, etc.

WORK HARD: Walk the talk. If you truly honor a strong work ethic, the image will take care of itself. People naturally gain respect for someone who works hard. This doesn't mean you have to exhaust yourself going 90 miles an hour day and night. If you do that, you'll be on a collision course with burn out—physical and mental. You'll soon lose the respect of others and become ineffective on the job. Balance is the key. This means putting in an honest day's work for a day's pay. Think about this. If you were paying your own pay check, would you be getting your money's worth? If you can answer "yes," then you're doing O.K.

BUILD TRUST: Trust is the foundation of a strong counseling program. Teachers, students, administrators, and parents must know that you say what you mean and mean what you say. They must know they can depend on you to honor confidentiality. They must respect your skills and trust your ability to handle sensitive situations. They must see you "walk the talk," "practice what you preach," and follow through with what you promise.

EVALUATE: Take time to do an annual evaluation of your program. Survey a sampling of all audiences you serve—parents, teachers, students, administrators, support staff. Assess school needs and adjust your services accordingly within the guidelines of your district or state guidance plan. A sample evaluation survey is included at the end of this chapter.

Points to Remember
Chapter 3

1. Expect the unexpected on the first few days of school.
2. Make time for DOCUMENTATION.
3. Join professional organizations and get familiar with legal and ethical codes of conduct.
4. Avoid OVERLOAD by scheduling workable numbers of individuals and groups.
5. Invest time in promoting positive public relations.
6. Build trust through honoring confidentiality.

TEACHER REFERRAL FOR COUNSELING

Student _____ Homeroom _____

Referral Source_____ Date _____

Reason for referral:

_____ Poor peer relationships
_____ Behavioral problems
_____ Academic problems
_____ Family changes (death, divorce, re-marriage, moving, etc.)
_____ Extremely withdrawn
_____ Doesn't accept responsibility
_____ Sudden changes in mood, attitude, or behavior
_____ Other

Special services student is receiving _____

List any interventions/assistance you have offered to the student _____
_____
_____

Do you have a preference as to time of guidance appointment? _____

I would like for my student to be able to: _____
_____

FIGURE 3-2

Menu
for single parents

Volume I, Issue 3
Flowertown Elementary

Janet M. Bender, M.Ed.
School Counselor

—Appetizer—

We are all sometimes critical of our own parenting abilities. We feel guilty if we do too much or too little, if we're too strict or too lenient with our children. Every parent has these thoughts from time to time. If we are to have peace of mind, we need to forgive ourselves for our imperfections and mistakes. We all do the best we can with what we know at the time. As you learn more about being a parent, your confidence will grow. As you grow, your children will grow more secure and your relationship with your children will be a healthy, rewarding one for you both. So, relax and be the best parent you can be.

—Entree—

Boundaries

A boundary is defined as a "limit" or "border". Familiar visual boundaries are physical borders such as fences, walls and painted lines on highways and tennis courts. The purpose of a boundary is to limit behavior or action within a certain acceptable area or space. Boundaries are necessary to protect the safety and well-being of the animal or person living within them. They also help define the order and values of our society.

What does all this have to do with parents and children? Just as boundaries make our world a safer and more civilized place in which to live, boundaries within a family help our children feel more secure and behave more appropriately. Defining adult/children boundaries is especially difficult in single-parent families. Children who are elevated to an equal level with their parent share the power and authority of that parent. This results in confusion about expectations for behavior. When this happens, the family operates in chaos, much like a tennis match without boundary lines or a net to divide the court. Imagine a highway without a center line or speed limit. Without limits, the people operating in these situations would become out of control, frustrated, and unsafe.

(Continued on next page)

Boundaries

So, how do you establish healthy boundaries within your family? Keep these thoughts in mind:

1. Remind yourself regularly that you are the parent and it's your job to be "in charge".

2. Don't try to compensate for the absent parent by being your child's "buddy".

3. Communicate clearly your expectations for behavior.

4. Enforce physical boundaries. (Children sleep in their own beds, wear seat belts, play within a designated area, watch only children's tv shows, etc.)

5. Avoid putting young children "in charge" of younger siblings. This gives them an unrealistic sense of power which may carry over into the parent/child relationship.

6. Find an adult friend or counselor to talk with so your child doesn't become a confidant or adult replacement. Let your child be a child.

7. Consistently follow through with natural and logical consequences for misbehavior. Children need the security of firm discipline/teaching even when they seem unhappy about it.

8. Expect resistance and emotional opposition to the limits you set. It's normal for children to test boundaries.

9. Remain calm while enforcing consequences of boundary violations. Don't give in to whining or emotional displays of anger.

10. Acknowledge your mistakes and keep trying.

—Kids' Menu—

Plan with your children, recreational activities that are free or inexpensive. Families that have fun together will develop a positive regard for each other. City parks are excellent for picnics, playgrounds, and tennis. Libraries, museums, bike rides, or hikes can provide educational and fun outings. Feeding ducks or birds leftover bread crumbs can be fun. Even tossing a football or frisbee® in the yard is quality and free recreation for all. Don't rely on television as a baby-sitter, entertainer and educator. Plan some time for exercise and outdoor activities.

—Dessert—

"Today is the tomorrow you worried about yesterday".

"Don't let the seeds spoil your enjoyment of a watermelon.
Just spit out the seeds".

End of Year Evaluation and Needs Assessment of Elementary Guidance Program

In order to evaluate our program and plan for next year, we need your input. Please rate your degree of satisfaction with the following guidance services. Fee free to add comments if needed.

E=Excellent   A=Adequate   N=Needs more emphasis

____ 1. The counselor orients students, teachers, and parents to the guidance services available at the school.

____ 2. The counselor works with individual students as needed.

____ 3. The counselor provides small group guidance and counseling for students with similar concerns.

____ 4. The counselor conducts interesting and relevant classroom guidance lessons on a regular basis.

____ 5. The counselor conducts follow-up consultation with teachers, parents and administrators who have referred students.

____ 6. The counselor utilizes outside agencies and services when needed. (Mental Health, DSS, Hospice, etc.).

____ 7. The counselor works cooperatively with all staff members.

____ 8. The counselor provides for parent education/support through workshops, newsletters, and conferences.

____ 9. The counselor assists students in making the transition from school to school through orientation activities (new students, school visits, etc.).

____ 10. The counselor responds to emergency referrals appropriately and in a timely manner.

____ 11. The counselor coordinates school-wide programs and services (testing, SST, Red Ribbon, Just Say No, etc.).

____ 12. The counselor maintains a library of pertinent materials and information and makes them available to students, staff and parents.

____ 13. The counselor is prompt and dependable for appointments and other duties.

____ 14. What would you consider the strengths of our guidance program?

_____

____ 15. What additional services, programs, emphases would you like to see next year?

_____

Grade _____   Name (optional) _____

CHAPTER 4

Individual Counseling

You've already received skill training in the goal-directed helping process of counseling. Now it is time to put into practice what you have learned. In the elementary school, individual counseling should be limited to short term interventions whenever possible. With a case load of 400-600 students, it is not efficient to spend a major portion of your time seeing individual students. In an average school year, I see approximately 150-200 individual students for an average of 4-5 sessions each. The number of visits might range from one to twelve. It is a rare occasion when I meet continuously throughout the year with a student. I only have one or two of those each year. In most cases the student resolves his/her problem within a few sessions, or I invite the student to participate in a small group or make an outside referral if necessary.

Individual sessions may range from ten minutes to forty minutes once or twice a week, depending on the age of the child and the severity of the situation. My sessions are usually between twenty and thirty minutes in duration and meet once a week except for emergency interventions which may require daily monitoring for a short time. Separation anxiety, behavior intervention/reinforcement, and abuse cases are examples of emergencies that may require your attention more often than once a week.

Breaking the Ice

Elementary aged children are by nature friendly and trusting. Rapport is usually easy to establish in a matter of seconds with students who have self-referred. For more reluctant students, there are a number of ice breaker behaviors on the part of the counselor that can help build rapport quickly.

1. Introduce the child to a puppet friend.
2. Invite the child to explore your play area.
3. Comment genuinely on the child's shoes, bracelet, etc.
4. Offer the child art paper and crayons or paint.
5. Invite the child to play a game with you.
6. Avoid asking questions right away.
7. Ask the child to help you with a task. (sorting toys, putting up a bulletin board, etc.)
8. Read a story to the child.
9. Take a walk on the playground.
10 "Getting to Know You" sentence starters (orally or written)

Once you've "broken the ice," you may need to set a timer to indicate the ending of the session. Most students enjoy being with the counselor and will stay as long as you let them. I started using a timer with a child who had great difficulty respecting limits and boundaries in any setting. I allowed her to take control of helping me set the timer and she gradually made progress terminating sessions without it.

What Can We Do Besides Talk?

If you are like me, much of my counseling training was in techniques that involved talking and listening to the client. Some young children and some people of any age may not be very verbally expressive. That's OK. A lot of helping and healing can take place without a lot of talking. The following is a list of activities that can be used with individual children. Details of some of these follow at the end of this chapter.

1. Use of props and magic tricks.
2. Art activities such as: family drawing, animal you'd like to be, self-portrait, scribble pictures, lines of feelings, play-doh® sculptures, etc.
3. Cooperative games: feelings cube (toss a feeling and share),Ungame®, Go Fishing (questions about self on fish), Caterpillar Game
4. Puppets/role play/pretend
5. Music/ fingerplays
6. Make-believe/ making wishes with wand or Aladdin's lamp,cloud pictures
7. Storytelling/ child tells and counselor writes, child illustrates
8. Bibliotherapy/ read and discuss story with similar theme as the child's issue.
9. Non-directive play with appropriate counselor validation (Play Therapy: The Art of the Relationship, Gary L. Landreth)

Getting to Know You!

1. My favorite food is _____.

2. If I had three wishes, I would wish for:

   _____

   _____

   _____

3. I am good at _____.

4. I feel bad when _____.

5. I don't like _____.

6. If I were principal of my school, I would _____

   _____.

7. Something you probably don't know about me is _____

   _____.

8. I would like to learn to: _____.

9. I like it when my teacher _____.

10. I worry about: _____

    _____.

Name _____

FIGURE 4-2

Feelings Cube

Use the cube pattern below and make a construction paper cube. Have the child toss the cube, think about the feeling word that lands faceup, and tell about a time when he or she had that feeling.

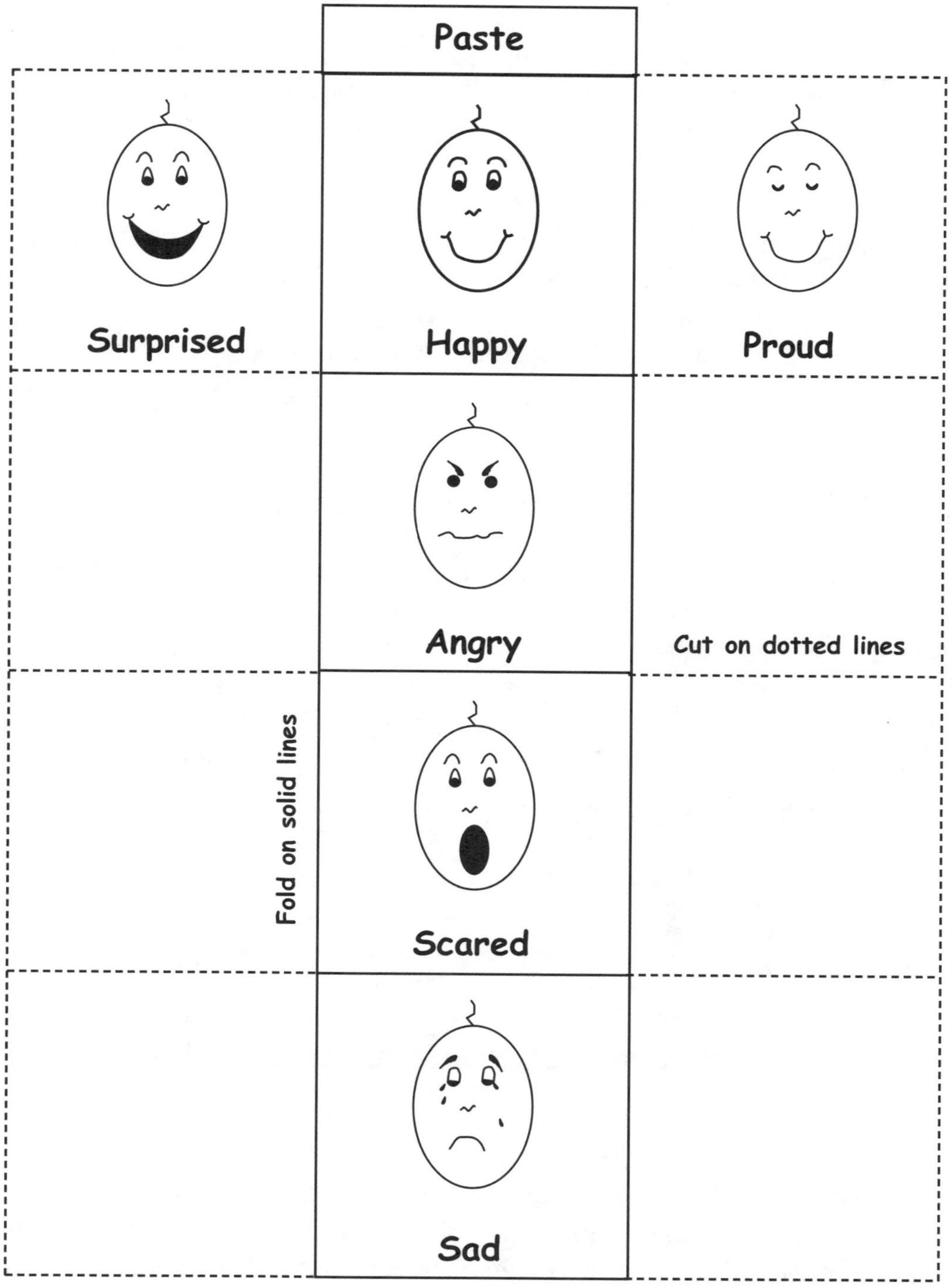

Paste

Surprised

Happy

Proud

Angry

Cut on dotted lines

Fold on solid lines

Scared

Sad

Confidentiality

When working with elementary children, confidentiality is rarely supported by legal precedent. In other words, in a court of law (in S.C.), there is no real confidentiality for elementary school counselors. Be sure to familiarize yourself with the laws in your state. It is sometimes a balancing act to protect the rights of the child as your client while operating within the legal rights of the parents. It is important to maintain the trust of the child by being honest with him/her when you feel it necessary to contact a parent. If I think it is important or imperative for the parent to be involved, I discuss it with the child and get his/her permission before contacting the parent. I feel comfortable asking parents to allow me some latitude in confidentiality with their child in order to gain the child's trust. This is not usually a problem in cases where parents make the referral to you. This is a time when positive public relations efforts and orientation for parents can pay off in parent trust and support for the counselor. Of course, if a child is in danger himself or to others, legal precedents overrule this ethical decision.

Beyond the parent, you should maintain a reasonable degree of confidentiality within the school environment. A rule of thumb I use is the "need to know" test. I weigh the welfare of the child with the need of the classroom teacher or administrator to know essential facts and then carefully consult accordingly. I have at times had parents entrust me with private information that they insist should remain private to protect their child. It is very important to respect these requests unless it is a violation of law. In any case, it is never appropriate to have a teachers' lounge discussion about a student's private concerns. Maintaining a helping, trusting relationship with students is vital to the success of your program.

Outside Referrals

As a school counselor, you will be a liaison between the school and many outside agencies. Consult with veteran counselors in your district and form a list of community agencies and phone numbers for quick reference. In our district, we include this list in our

Counselors' Calendar. Mental Health, Department of Social Services, Alcohol Commission, Hospice, etc. are few of the commonly needed agencies. A list of area private and public counselors would also be helpful.

It is important to realize your boundaries and limitations as a school counselor to avoid **Pothole # 8: ENMESHMENT** In your desire to help all students, you may find yourself becoming over involved personally, or emotionally frustrated when you can't achieve the results you desire for a student or family. Your level of training, your case load of students, and your guidance program guidelines, will make it necessary and prudent to refer students and their parents at times to outside agencies. Knowing when to let go  is an important lesson that comes with experience and self examination. Sometimes the best way to help a student is to lead him/her to another source for help. After you have seen a student three or four times, assess the situation, decide if you can provide the help he needs, and if not, refer to another source such as the school student assistance team or appropriate outside agency. Generally, school counselors provide short term counseling and consultation. If extensive family counseling appears to be needed, provide for the parent a list of several possible providers in the area. You can still follow-up on the student's progress through consultation with the new service provider. Be sure to have the parent sign a release form which allows consultation between professionals.

As you get to know area counselors and social workers, you will develop a valuable network of professionals. A team approach promotes positive public relations and provides more effective services for students and their families. Some school districts are fortunate to have school-based social workers/family counselors who work intensively with a few families. Utilize these people when available.

If you do not already know, quickly familiarize yourself with the laws and policies in your state regarding the reporting of suspected child abuse and neglect. Child protection laws vary from state to state. It is your responsibility to inform staff members on recognizing and reporting suspected incidents. Again, talk with your district chairperson or a veteran counselor about district policies and procedures.

Closure

In a school setting, termination/closure of individual counseling may be planned or it may be unexpected. Students sometimes move in and out of schools with little or no notice. Often these highly mobile students are the ones you will be seeing for counseling. For this reason, I try to end each session in a way that prepares the child to cope on his/her own whether or not we meet again. It is helpful to review feelings, goals, successes and leave the child looking forward to seeing you again, but at the same time prepared to cope successfully if for some reason he/she does not come back. I rarely make a permanent closure unless I know a student is moving away. Otherwise, I will temporarily end our meetings when goals have been reached, with an open invitation for the student to self-refer again if it becomes necessary.

Points to Remember
Chapter 4

1. Establishing rapport with students doesn't always require a lot of talking. Try a variety of strategies.
2. Maintain confidentiality with students' private concerns.
3. Involve parents when needed or required by local law or policy.
4. Accept your limitations, and prevent ENMESHMENT with clients by making outside referrals when necessary.

Possible Indicators of Child Abuse and Neglect

The following is a partial list of possible physical and behavioral indicators that MAY mean a child is being abused or neglected.

Possible Indicators of Physical Abuse

❑ Unexplained bruises or welts
❑ Unexplained burns
❑ Unexplained fractures
❑ Unexplained cuts or scrapes
❑ Unexplained stomach injuries
❑ Unexplained visual or hearing defects

❑ Human bite marks
❑ Fear of Adults
❑ Overly aggressive or withdrawn
❑ Frightened of parents
❑ Afraid to go home
❑ School problems

Possible Indicators of Physical Neglect

❑ Underfed or constantly hungry
❑ Constantly unclean
❑ Lack of supervision
❑ Unattended medical needs
❑ Growth rate below normal

❑ Begging or stealing food
❑ Constantly tired
❑ Poor school attendance
❑ Drug or alcohol problems

Possible Indicators of Sexual Abuse

❑ Difficulty in walking or sitting
❑ Pain or itching around genitals
❑ Stomach aches
❑ Bed-wetting
❑ Sleep problems

❑ Depression or withdrawn behavior
❑ Poor peer relationships
❑ Sudden onset of behavior problems
❑ Unusual knowledge of or interest in sex

Possible Indicators of Emotional/Psychological Abuse

❑ Speech problems
❑ Slow physical growth
❑ Slow mental or emotional growth
❑ Habit of sucking, biting, or rocking
❑ Antisocial or destructive behavior
❑ Loss of appetite

❑ Long-term depression
❑ Sexual acting out
❑ Sleep problems
❑ Dramatic emotional swings
❑ Suicide attempts
❑ Learning difficulties

Source: "Understanding Child Abuse and Neglect" The William Gladden Foundation, York, PA. 17404

Symptoms of Neglect and Psychological Abuse

The following is a partial list of symptoms which appear to indicate neglect and psychological child abuse. These forms of child abuse are especially dangerous to the child's self-esteem and can cause long-term psychological, emotional, and social problems that may remain with the child into adulthood.

- ❑ Teasing or "putting down" child
- ❑ Yelling or screaming at child
- ❑ Deserting or avoiding child
- ❑ Disinterest in or rejection of child
- ❑ Constant criticism of child
- ❑ Calling child bad names
- ❑ Threatening to harm child
- ❑ Blaming child for situations not within his/her control
- ❑ Withholding love, affection or attention
- ❑ Withholding food
- ❑ Withholding medical attention
- ❑ Failing to meet the child's physical and emotional needs
- ❑ Isolating the child from society or "normal" friendships
- ❑ Negatively comparing the child with other children
- ❑ "Setting-up" the child to fail
- ❑ Embarrassing the child in public
- ❑ Often making the child feel ashamed or guilty
- ❑ Using the child as a "weapon" in separation or divorce
- ❑ Dressing the child in clothes of the opposite sex
- ❑ Teaching the child immoral or illegal behaviors
- ❑ Lying to the child
- ❑ Sharing dangerous drugs or alcohol with the child
- ❑ Stealing the child from his/her other natural parent
- ❑ Placing the child in dangerous situations
- ❑ Keeping the child out of school

CHAPTER 5

Road map to Small Groups

Group Dynamics

As a school counselor, facilitating student growth in small groups is one of the most rewarding aspects of my job. It also makes sense to maximize student contact by working with several students at a time.

The group process, when it works well, is a powerful therapeutic experience for children. In his book, A Survival Guide for the Elementary/Middle School Counselor, John Schmidt discusses group counseling as an essential service of a comprehensive school counseling program which results in the outcome of students helping each other.

Counseling groups in the elementary school are usually best organized around a topic of interest or need to several students within the same grade level.

Setting Up Groups

Once you have identified 3-6 students with similar concerns or needs, you are ready to conduct small group counseling. Refer to the master schedule and your classroom guidance schedule to find a time that will work for all participants. I schedule 30- minute sessions once a week for six to eight weeks. I send out a permission note to parents and a group notice to teachers and students about a week or so before the group begins. Sometimes a phone call to parents is necessary to prompt the return of permission forms. I ask permission for all groups involving personal concerns. Guidance groups such as study skills, new students, etc. do not require getting parental permission. Even after giving out group notices, you'll probably still have to retrieve students from their classrooms when it's time for their group to meet. For safety and supervision reasons, it is best to walk younger children to and from their classrooms. Allow extra time in your schedule for this.

Types, Duration, Frequency

There are two types of small groups...small group guidance and small group counseling. Small group guidance refers to groups which address primarily informational issues. Examples of group guidance would be new student welcome groups and study skills groups. Counseling groups are more focused on developmental and emotional issues that students need to process. Groups for children of divorce or grief/loss groups fit into this category. It should be mentioned here that often there is overlap between these two types. Even in a new student welcome group with a set agenda, an individual student may introduce feelings about moving which evolve into a counseling exchange. Guidance groups can often be a source of referrals for future counseling groups as issues are disclosed.

There are also three kinds of counseling groups: topical, developmental, and ongoing support groups. Most new counselors would be wise to start with topical groups and grow into the others as you become more experienced. Topics will be dictated by the needs in your school. I have found Families in Transition, Grief/Loss, Self-Esteem, and Peer Relations to be popular topics.

What about the duration time of small groups? In the school setting, I have found that 6-10 sessions work well for me with the average group running 8 weeks. You can meet once a week for 6-10 weeks, or you can meet twice a week for half the time. Sometimes I start out with a plan to meet 8 weeks, then find that a group needs more or less time depending on their progress. I believe that it is best to begin with one meeting a week. Teachers may be more cooperative about letting you pull students from class if the instructional time missed is limited. John Schmidt addresses "selling group counseling" in his aforementioned book. Certain topics may lend themselves to the bi-weekly schedule such as retention groups, or groups started only three or four weeks before a lengthy holiday. Also groups with kindergarten children work well meeting twice a week. How long should a group session last? This too, varies depending upon the developmental level of the child and the school schedule. A group may meet for 20 minutes up to 40 minutes. I usually plan to meet with my groups for 30 minutes allowing a few minutes between groups for transition.

The Group Process

Once you've sent out forms and letters, plan your group activities. Never try to "wing it" with a new group. A workable outline for group procedure is:

1. Introductions, group rules, brief overview (Name Game is fun.)
2. Icebreaker or energizer activity (game, art activity, etc.)
3. Discussion of activity (Processing)
4. Closure (Success cards, stickers, etc.)

To help students bond with each other and gain some ownership of the group, I make time during the first session to let them choose a group name and success card which suits them. They usually brainstorm and come to consensus, but sometimes it comes down to a vote. Some names my groups have chosen are: Footlockers, Sweethearts, Cool Bees, etc. I have included samples of several success card patterns I use, but you can enlarge any clip art picture or drawing and add boxes for stickers.

There are many books in print which provide "cookbook" small group activities. I usually prefer putting together my own lesson plans from a variety of sources. The important thing is to get the students actively involved and thinking while forming positive relationships. Activities are a catalyst to promote growth and learning. If the students are having fun, they will want to return. If they are learning about themselves and others, you are facilitating personal growth. It will take time to learn how to plan and work within your 30 minute time frame. Try not to attempt to do too much and end up rushing students and yourself to get back to class on time. Teachers will appreciate your efforts to stay within the designated time.

Group Activities and Materials

There are countless numbers of activities and materials you can use with groups. This section is not intended to cover those at length. I suggest reviewing and buying one or two good group activity books to get you started. One of my favorite ones is Child Support Through Small Group Counseling, by Lois Landy. There are also several helpful group resources offered through Youthlight, Inc. and Marco Publishing.

In preparing for small groups, there are a few props and materials that I find helpful in working with elementary students. You may want to begin collecting these as you can.

1. Beanbags for taking turns talking and for group juggling.
2. Feelings Cube (a cube with different feelings faces on each side), feelings puppets, feelings pictures to facilitate sharing of feelings
3. Magic wand or lamp for making wishes
4. Crayons and art paper, scissors, glue, construction paper (any art supplies)
5. Magnetic fishing game
6. Soft building blocks
7. Play-Doh® or modeling clay
8. Miniature toy animals, people figures and puppets
9. Hand mirrors

Additionally, you may begin setting up a group notebook on common topics: families in transition (divorce, remarriage, stepfamilies, single parents), grief/loss, friendship/peer relations, anger management, study skills, self-esteem, coping with illness in the family, etc.

Points to Remember
Chapter 5

1. Small group counseling is a dynamic helping process.
2. Identify students for small groups with similar concerns. (Start with one or two groups.)
3. Schedule times.
4. Get parental permission for personal topics.
5. Limit groups to workable numbers (3-7).
6. Plan weekly activities.
7. Keep attendance records and summaries of activities. (Sample form included.)

FIGURE 5-1

Dear Parent,

As part of our school's developmental guidance program, some students are invited to participate in small group counseling sessions. Children who share a common concern, meet together with the counselor to receive support through talking, learning and sharing. Participation in these groups is voluntary.

I am inviting your child, _____ to participate in a small group for 30 minutes a week for 6-8 weeks. The topic will be: _____

The group will begin shortly after I receive all permission forms. Activities may include artwork, games, discussion, filmstrips, or stories that encourage individual expression of feelings and teach positive coping skills. Confidentiality of personal information is respected.

If you have any questions or specific concerns, feel free to call me at _____. I look forward to working with your child. Please sign and return the form below to insure your child's placement in the group.

Sincerely,

_____
School Counselor

- -

I would like for my child, _____ to receive support through participation in small group counseling.

_____   _____
Parent/Guardian   Date

Please clip and return to school.

FIGURE 5-2
Sample Small Group Counseling Schedule

Times	Monday	Tuesday	Wednesday	Thursday	Friday
8:00-8:30					
8:30-9:00					
9:00-9:30					
9:30-10:00					
10:00-10:30					
10:30-11:00					
11:00-11:30					
11:30-12:00					
12:00-12:30					
12:30-1:00					
1:00-1:30					
1:30-2:00					

Just wanted to remind
you that Pat's Pals will
be meeting in your pod
on _____

at_____.

See you then!!

Small Group Counseling

Student _____

Teacher _____

Date _____ Time _____

FIGURE 5-4

Small Group Guidance

To: _____

The following students from your class are invited to attend a small group on study skills.

Meeting day: _____ at _____ beginning _____.

I will come to your room to pick up these students.

Thank you!

_____

_____

_____

_____

_____

FIGURE 5-5

Memo: Classroom Teachers
From:
Date:
Re: Guidance Support for Repeaters

To help make retention a more positive experience for

_____, I plan to:

1. Work with and support parents to help them deal positively with their child.

2. Work in small groups with students who are repeating to help them better understand and deal with retention.

3. Provide leadership opportunities and enrichment experiences for repeating students to build their confidence and self-esteem.

I will be meeting in small groups with first grade repeaters on

_____ at _____ beginning

_____ for three consecutive weeks.

Please let me know how these students are adjusting and if they need further support from me.

Thanks,

Dear _____,

At _____, we realize that repeating a grade brings forth mixed feelings in a child and his/her family.

As your child's guidance counselor, I want to work with you to assure a successful experience this year for your child _____.

My primary concern is that your child have a positive attitude toward school and about him/herself.

To help make the retention a more positive experience, I plan to:

1. Work with and support parents to help them deal positively with their child.

2. Work in small groups with students who are repeating to help them better understand and deal with retention.

3. Provide leadership opportunities and enrichment experiences for repeating students to build their confidence and self-esteem.

Thank you for your support of your child. I have enclosed two articles that I hope will be helpful. Please call on me if I can be of further assistance to you or your child.

Sincerely,

Guidance Counselor

FIGURE 5-7

Group Counseling Summary Sheet

Topic ______________________________ **Meeting Times** ____________________

Participants	Class	Attending Sessions									
		1	2	3	4	5	6	7	8	9	10

Dates **Activities Completed**

____

____

____

____

____

____

____

____

____

FIGURE 5-8

Success Card For

Name

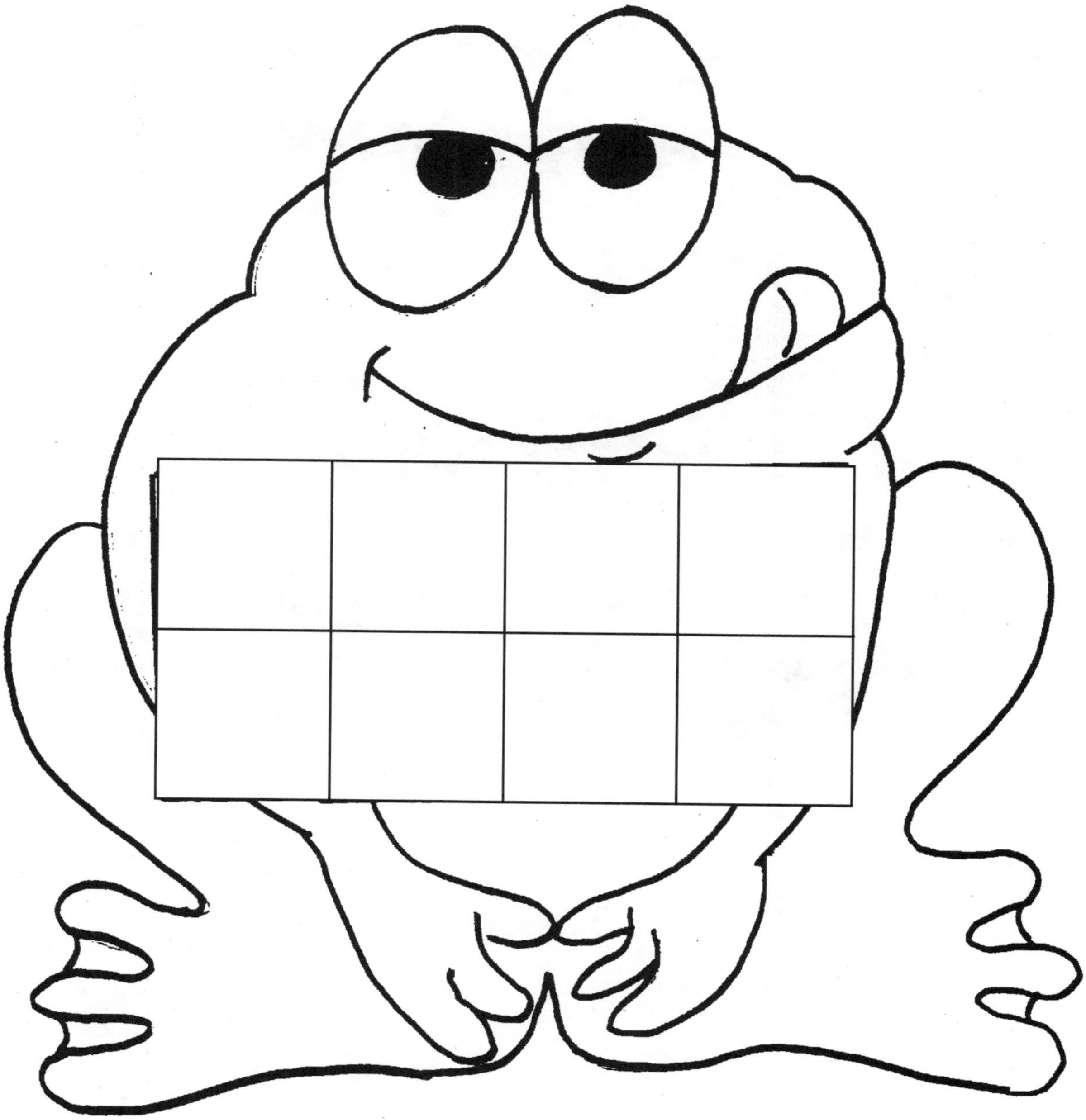

Success Card For

_____

Success Card For

_____

Name

Success Card For

Name _____

CHAPTER 6

On The Road With Classroom Guidance

Regularly scheduled classroom guidance lessons taught by the counselor can be the "chassis" through which you transmit the message and energy of your entire program. Classroom guidance serves two main purposes. It provides: 1) an opportunity to teach students developmentally appropriate life skills, and 2) a forum for getting acquainted with students and their needs.

It is preferable for classroom teachers to observe your lessons and provide daily reinforcement and follow up on the skills taught. Especially in the case of a school-wide emphasis such as conflict management, the teacher's participation and involvement is vital to the success of the program. Additionally, the teacher's presence enables him/her to give you helpful feedback on your program.

Classroom guidance also provides an excellent opportunity for you to model positive communication with students and an open exchange of feelings and opinions. Make your lessons creative and interesting. Active involvement by students is a must. You'll know you're on the right track if students greet your visits with positive comments or even applause.

Rules of the Road

As I stated earlier, the counselor should not be seen by students as a disciplinarian. For this reason, classroom teachers should remain with their classes during classroom guidance time. I let teachers know about this expectation at orientation time. The classroom climate can be a little more relaxed than some teachers allow during their teaching time, but the basic classroom rules should still apply. It is extremely important to get off to a good start by clearly communicating your expectations to teachers and students. The most important rule to agree upon is mutual respect between and among students and instructor.

How to Put on the Brakes with a Runaway Classroom

You can expect to have one or two classes that exhibit challenging behaviors. It may be due to ineffective classroom management on the part of the regular teacher, or it may be when a teacher leaves the room during your lesson. In either case, it helps to have a few tricks up your sleeve to handle the situation.

1. Use silence/waiting for their attention.
2. Use hand signals or sign language. (Stop. Look. Listen.)
3. Use a shy turtle puppet who is afraid to come out until all is quiet.
4. Reward students for appropriate behavior with warm fuzzies, stickers, "cool bee" cutouts, etc. (I keep a pocket full for emergencies.)
5. Involve students actively, lecture less.
6. Enlist students to help with lesson. (Choose attentive ones and comment on it.)
7. Use lots of positive reinforcement. "Give yourself a pat on the back for being a good listener. Thank you."

The following are sample classroom guidance lessons that I have used. I have selected lessons which require a minimum of materials...many using literature from the school library. I often use an easy magic trick or puppet introduction to set up the lesson. Feel free to use them or adapt them to your needs.

CLASSROOM GUIDANCE

ACTIVITY

TOPIC: Self-Awareness
TITLE: "The Me You Don't See"
LEVEL: K-3rd (I've used with 1st)
MATERIALS: 2 wrapped packages, one containing something undesirable like a crushed empty soda can...the other a desirable gift such as individually wrapped pieces of candy. Wrap the large, undesirable gift in pretty paper with a bow. Wrap the small nice gift in newspaper or other plain, ugly wrapping. The Me You Don't See worksheet for each student, crayons.

PROCEDURE: Inform the class that you brought them a class gift. Discuss possible contents of the boxes. " What do you think might be in this box? This one?" Ask the students if they can tell what is inside the boxes by looking at the outside. Ask: "How do you find out what is inside a package?" Have the class take a vote on which package they want for the class gift. Then set gifts aside telling them, "We will open your class gift later."

Ask: "Do people come in packages?" If the answer is "no," then say: "Well let me describe my "wrapping." I am sort of tall with short blonde hair, blue eyes, fair skin with freckles, and I'm wearing a black skirt and jacket, etc." Then allow several volunteers to describe their outward packages. Then ask: "Is there another person in the world that looks just like you? Why not? What if you had a twin?" (No, even twins have some small differences.)

Say: "You told me earlier that you would have to open the gifts to find out what was inside. How do you find out what a person is like on the inside? (talk to, get to know, watch their behavior) In school, in your neighborhood, in your family, you have to learn to get along with lots of different people. It helps us to get along better if we remember that people are all different on the outside and the inside. We are UNIQUE. We can be different and still be friends and classmates."

"Let's take a few minutes to share what's inside our 'gift wrapping'." Give every student a worksheet and ask them to draw and color pictures or write words to tell us things about themselves that we can't see on the outside. Suggest telling about things they like to do, interest they have, subjects they like in school, etc. With younger children, you may want to show them your completed worksheet as an example. Circulate around the room and interact with students as they work. If time permits, let several students share their interests with the class. Encourage the teacher to display drawings with students' permission.

Optional adaptation: With older students, the class can brainstorm jobs and careers related to the interests and abilities drawn on their "Me You Don't See" worksheet.

At end of lesson time, open the class gift that students selected and discuss. (Every first grade class I have asked, has chosen the large, pretty package.) The class may want to see what is inside the other package. Use its contents to further reinforce these points.

Ask the children what they have learned from this lesson as far as people are concerned. Be sure these ideas come out:

1. People are different/UNIQUE.
2. We must take time to get to know a person before we know what he/she is like on the inside.
3. If we judge people only by their outer "wrapping,s" we might make a mistake and miss out on something good.

Close by asking the students if they have ever decided they didn't like someone when they first met them, only to change their minds after getting to know them. Allow time for sharing. Encourage them to remember what was learned from the lesson as they meet new people. (You can't judge a book by its cover.)

* *Adapted from Individual Differences: An Experience in Human Relations for Children, Madison Public Schools, Madison, Wisconsin, 1981.*

"The Me You Don't See"

_____

Name

ACTIVITY

CLASSROOM GUIDANCE

TOPIC: Peer Relations/Interpersonal Skills
LEVEL: K-4th
TITLE: Heart-to-Heart Communication

MATERIALS: Heart-shaped pillow with one red side and one purple side, toy figure of a man, soldier and tank, boy or girl puppet, appropriate level handout for each student.

PROCEDURE: Show children your pillow and ask them what a heart makes you think of. (love, caring) Yes, and today we are going to learn how to talk to each other in a caring way so we will get along without hurting each others feelings... heart-to-heart communication.

Tell students this story: Once there was a man who went to war. What is a war? (a conflict between two or more countries) Yes, a war is when people or countries fight each other. Mr. _____went to war in a faraway land. One day he was wounded. What does wounded mean? Yes, it is when someone is shot or injured in such a way that they need a doctor. Mr. _____ was hurt so badly that he couldn't do his job in the war anymore. When he got back home to his country, he was given a medal for being so brave during the war. The medal was called a "Purple Heart Medal." This is a medal given to soldiers who are wounded while fighting in a war. Show heart pillow again. Tell students to notice that one side of pillow is red...we'll call this the happy heart. The other side is purple...we'll call this the wounded or hurting heart. Tell students that we're not in a war now, but that sometimes the words we say and the way we act can cause others to feel happy or sad. Happy feelings give us a red or happy heart. Sad or hurt feelings give us a purple or hurting heart. What kind of behaviors could cause someone to have hurt feelings? (teasing, bossing, name-calling, etc.)

Ask students, "Which would you rather have...a happy heart or a hurting heart?" (Flip pillow over to show each color as you talk.) Hopefully they will answer "a happy heart." Say: "Me too! We're going to practice ways to talk to each other that help us have a happy heart."

Introduce your puppet friend. "Boys and girls, this is my new friend, Etta Sue. Can you say something to her to make her feel welcome in your class? " As students raise hands to talk to puppet, hand them your pillow and have them hold it red side facing out as they speak to Etta Sue. After a few students have had a turn, say: "Now, Etta Sue, you give it a try." Tell these boys and girls something to give them happy hearts."

Etta Sue addresses several individual children saying nice things like:
"I like your smile."
"You have pretty hair."
"I'd like to play with you at recess."
Suddenly Etta Sue says: "You're weird!" to a student.
Quickly scold puppet by saying, "Etta Sue! That wasn't a happy heart message. That was a hurting heart message."

Puppet says, "I know. I was just kidding. I was just checking to see if ya'll were paying attention." Then to child she insulted: "I'm sorry, you're really nice." Compliment puppet: "That's better."

Review main points of lesson. OK, so when we want to get along with our friends, we use red or helping heart words. When we're having a problem getting along, we use purple or hurting heart words. We won't even talk about those words because we all know what they are...words that tease or call names or hurt feelings.

Give out worksheet and have students complete. Older students could write their own examples of "helping heart" and "hurting heart" phrases.

FIGURE 6-2

I'm a happy heart. Color me red.

I'm a hurting heart. Color me purple

"Happy Heart" words help people get along peacefully.

"Hurting Heart" words cause hurt feelings and conflict.

Color the hearts to show which are happy words and which are hurting words.

- "You better gimme that!"

- "I like you!"

- "I'm happy when you share with me."

- "You're mean!"

- "Thank you for sharing your crayons."

- "If you don't play with me I'll tell."

- "Please help me."

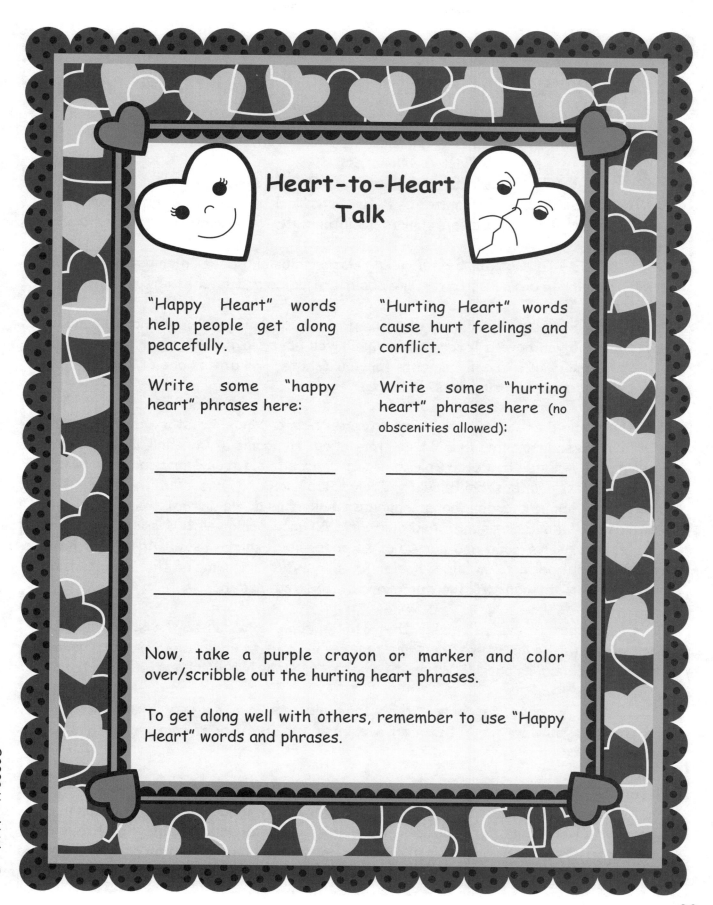

Heart-to-Heart Talk

"Happy Heart" words help people get along peacefully.

Write some "happy heart" phrases here:

_____

_____

_____

_____

"Hurting Heart" words cause hurt feelings and conflict.

Write some "hurting heart" phrases here (no obscenities allowed):

_____

_____

_____

_____

Now, take a purple crayon or marker and color over/scribble out the hurting heart phrases.

To get along well with others, remember to use "Happy Heart" words and phrases.

CLASSROOM GUIDANCE

ACTIVITY

TOPIC: Character Development/Respect
TITLE: Teammates
LEVEL: 5th

MATERIALS: Story, Teammates by Peter Golenbock; word and definition cards for prejudice, justice, segregation, vigilante,& intimidate; one baseball card per student (optional).

OBJECTIVE: To promote better peer relationships and develop empathy for others by hearing and discussing a story about prejudice and friendship.

PROCEDURE: Ask: "How many of you enjoy either playing or watching baseball or softball? Do you have a favorite team? If you have played any sport, think about one of the most exciting movements for you. (share) What was one of the saddest or most embarrassing moments?" (share)

Tell the students that you would like to read them a wonderful story that has both exciting and sad moments in it. It's a story about the game of baseball and it's called Teammates, written by Peter Golenbock. It is based on a true story about two well-known professional baseball players, Jackie Robinson and "Pee Wee" Reese. This is also a story about change. Change happens to all of us as we grow. It happens to our families and in our community and our world. Change brings with it a lot of different feelings...some good and some not so good. For example, say, "All of you have feelings about going to middle school next year. What are some of the feelings that often come with change?" (scared, nervous, excited, sad, happy)

"It's important for us to realize that other people experience the same feelings that we do. (although not at the same time) Being able to understand someone else's feelings is called 'empathy.' When it comes to feelings, we're all on the same team."

"This story is about a change that took place in our country over 50 years ago...before you were born...before I was born. It is a story of courage and justice (fairness) and of prejudice and hostility."

Before you read the story to the students, go over a few vocabulary words that they'll hear as you read. Have them see how many they know. (Have flash cards prepared with words and definitions for: prejudice, justice, segregation, vigilante, and intimidate.) Tape word cards up in front of room. Read one definition at a time and call on a student to match with the correct word.

Have the students listen as the story is read to see what can be learned about understanding others' feelings and how that can help us get along better with others. Let them know that all who listen and try to learn something new will be glad that they did.

Read and discuss story. Hand out a baseball trading card to all who participated in the lesson. Tell them they can keep or trade with a friend later.

intimidate

...to make afraid;
...to force with
threats.

CLASSROOM GUIDANCE

ACTIVITY

TOPIC: Responsibility/Study Skills
LEVEL: 1st-5th

MATERIALS: any puppet (script can be adapted to fit the animal), story, Do I Have To? Stacy Quigley or I'm in Charge or similar book on responsible behavior.

Open with this puppet skit.

Parrot Puppet: Hi, boys and girls.
Counselor: This is Rainbow. How are you today, Rainbow?
Puppet: Not so good.
Counselor: Why not? What's wrong?
Puppet: Well, my mom told me I have to clean my cage before I can go outside and play with my friend.
Counselor: And what did you say?
Puppet: I said, (whining) "Do I have to?"
Counselor: I've heard that before. How many of you boys and girls have said that at some time? (Take time to let students share chores they don't like to do.) And what did your mom say?
Puppet: She said, "Yes, you have to." So that's why I'm unhappy. I don't want to clean my stinky old cage, but I don't know what to do about it."
Counselor: Well, Rainbow, sometimes we all are asked to do things we'd rather not do. In fact, so many people feel the way you do that someone wrote a book about it.

Show book and introduce story. Read to class and discuss. Discuss main character's feelings about himself when he was and wasn't responsible. Put the word "pride" on the board and discuss.

Have students complete worksheet Being Responsible and take home.

©2003 YouthLight, Inc.

FIGURE 6-5

Being Responsible

Responsible means being in charge of something and doing it without having to be reminded.

You have responsibilities at home and at school. What are some of your responsibilities?

Draw pictures or write names to show who does these jobs at your house.

1. Washes the dishes.

   _____

2. Works in the yard.

   _____

3. Makes the bed.

   _____

4. Picks up toys.

   _____

5. Cooks meals.

   _____

6. Dusts furniture.

   _____

7. Sets the table.

   _____

8. Clears the table.

   _____

9. Takes out the trash.

   _____

10. Feeds the pets.

    _____

FIGURE 6-6

Sharing Household Chores

In order to feel a part of a family unit, everyone needs to make a contribution. Helping with the work that needs to be done is one way to contribute.

One fun alternative to permanently assigned chores is to list every small job that needs to be done on that particular day. Use a blank sheet of paper and put a blank line in front of each job that is listed. Then allow all family members, parents included, to take turns choosing a job until a name is in every blank. "Many hands make light work," and everyone shares in the responsibility and pride of a clean home.

Sample chore sheet:

_____ Scrub the tub.

_____ Scrub the sink.

_____ Sweep the kitchen.

_____ Vacuum the den.

_____ Windex® the bathroom mirror.

_____ Scrub the toilet.

_____ Dust the den furniture.

_____ Sweep the porch.

_____ Wipe the kitchen counter.

_____ Unload the dishwasher.

_____ Load the dishwasher.

Additionally, every family member is responsible for picking up or cleaning up his/her own personal messes, spaces, bed, etc.

From: Your Guidance Counselor

CLASSROOM GUIDANCE

ACTIVITY

TOPIC: Career Awareness
TITLE: Magic Carpet Ride into the Future
LEVEL: 4th and up
MATERIALS: About 5-6 posters/ each with a drawing of a magic carpet and the name of a career, one marker for each poster

PROCEDURE: Prepare posters ahead of time with drawing of a magic carpet and title them with interesting careers. Display them around the room. (If you want to reuse posters, laminate them and use wipe off markers or tape a plain sheet of white paper on the carpet.)

Give these directions to the group. "Look around the room. Pretend you are going to take a magic carpet ride into the future. Choose a career destination that you find appealing. After you go to your magic carpet group, select a leader for the group to be the recorder and write on the poster as the group brainstorms all the special reasons this particular career would be the most exciting or best. Pretend you are a salesman or recruiter trying to convince others why they should choose this career."

Allow approximately 10 minutes for the groups to make their lists. Ask the leaders to read aloud their groups responses. After all groups have shared, give participants an opportunity to move to another career destination if the presentation convinces them that the career is more interesting than their original choice. Then discuss these or your own questions:

1. Which careers were chosen by the most people?
2. How much changing of minds took place? Does this happen with real careers? (Yes, people change careers an average of 7 times in their lifetime.)
3. What did we learn about jobs and about each other?
4. What academic skills will be needed to do each job?

At the secondary level, the job choices may be related to the Holland Self-Directed Search categories.

* Adapted from: Foster, E.S. (1989). Energizers and Icebreakers. Minneapolis, MN: Educational Media Corp.

Career Interest

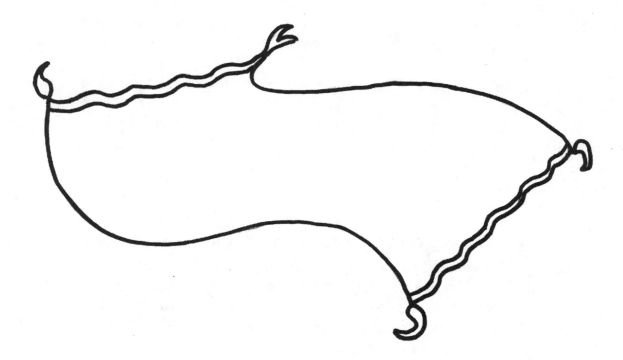

CLASSROOM GUIDANCE

ACTIVITY

TOPIC: Individual Differences
LEVEL: 1st-3rd
MATERIALS: Story, Elmer, by David McKee, drawing paper or pre-printed outline of elephant for each child, crayons

PROCEDURE: Ask students: "Are all people alike? Have you ever wished you were just like someone else? When? For what reasons?" (some reasons might be: to be popular, to get better grades, to fit in with a group)

Ask: "What would it be like if all people were exactly alike?" (discuss) "Today I would like to share a story with you about an elephant who felt unhappy because he was different from all the other elephants in the jungle. Listen to find ut why the other elephants laughed at Elmer."

Read story.

Discuss.
1. Why did the elephants laugh at Elmer? (he taught them jokes and games, he had a good personality) Were they making fun of him? (no)
2. Why did Elmer think they were laughing at him? (because he was different) Have you ever thought someone was making fun of or talking about you?
3. How did the elephants decide to celebrate the day of Elmer's best joke? (by decorating themselves in his honor)
4. Do you think Elmer learned anything about being different? (Yes, that being different isn't bad, but can be fun; and that personality and behavior deter mine one's popularity more than looks do.)
5. What are some ways that people are different from one another? (looks, learning ability, physical disabilities, etc.)
6. How should we treat people who are different from us? (with respect and kindness)

Culminating Activity: Ask children to design their own elephant for the Elmer's Day parade. No two should be alike.

CLASSROOM GUIDANCE

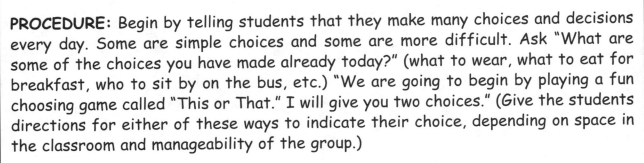

ACTIVITY

TOPIC: Decision-Making
TITLE: Rules of the Road
LEVEL: 2nd-5th (30-45 minute lesson)
MATERIALS: Draw a simple map of a typical neighborhood with several intersecting streets on the chalkboard or overhead transparency, 4 or 5 toy cars, 5 construction paper footprints with one of the decision-making steps written on each one, bathtub worksheet for each student (optional).

PROCEDURE: Begin by telling students that they make many choices and decisions every day. Some are simple choices and some are more difficult. Ask "What are some of the choices you have made already today?" (what to wear, what to eat for breakfast, who to sit by on the bus, etc.) "We are going to begin by playing a fun choosing game called "This or That." I will give you two choices." (Give the students directions for either of these ways to indicate their choice, depending on space in the classroom and manageability of the group.)

1. Show me "thumbs up" or "thumbs down." or
2. Move quietly to one side of the room or the other as I point out the choices.

Remind students to think for themselves, not to follow what their friends do. Some of the choices I give are:

> Are you more like...a banana or an orange?
> a rabbit or a turtle?
> a mouse or a lion?
> a bat or a ball?
> a give or a taker?
> inside or outside?

After each choice, allow one or two students to share their reason for their choice.

After this initial activity Tell the students that these were choices they made just for fun...simple choices. Sometimes they will have more difficult choices to make. In those cases they might need a plan for helping them figure out what to do. Today I'm going to teach you a plan for making choices.

Next ask: "Who thinks they can drive a car? Show the map you have put up in front of the room and toy cars. Choose 4 students at a time to come up and pretend to "drive their cars" along the streets any way they choose for about a minute or less. Continue with additional groups of 4 or so until everyone has a turn. Then ask:

"What happened?" "Were there any accidents?" What problems did you notice?" "What could make it safer to drive on these roads?" (Hopefully they will answer that we need rules.)

Have the class brainstorm "ways to make the roads safer." Add some traffic signs, speed limits, etc. to the map. Ask the students if they would agree that rules help make our roads after? Ask one group of four students to return to the map and "drive" their cars now with the road signs in place. Discuss the difference, (more order, and safer).

Say: "Just as brainstorming helped us solve the problem of dangerous roads, it can also help us when we have difficult decisions to make or problems to solve. Have you ever had a hard decision to make? (Hear a couple of examples.) I am going to share with you now 5 steps to help you make safe and wise decisions. Then we'll practice one of those steps, brainstorming." Go over the 5 steps below, taping up footsteps on the chalkboard as you discuss each one.

5 Steps to Making Decisions

1. Name the problem or question.
2. Brainstorm ideas/alternatives.
3. Think about the consequences of each idea.
4. Choose and do.
5. Check it out!

Refer back to one of the examples used earlier...ways to make roads safer, what to eat for breakfast, etc. if need to clarify. Be sure to point out that no one makes good decisions all the time., and that we can usually go back to step 4 and choose another option if the first choice doesn't work out well.

Optional extension activity: After you have discussed all the steps, review the brainstorming step by having students brainstorm aloud, "Ways to Use an Old Bathtub." Give each student a drawing of a bathtub and ask them to draw a unique way to use it. (You may incorporate "TALENTS" terminology, "Many varied and unusual ways to use an old bathtub.")

Review the 5 steps by handing out the paper footsteps to 5 students and asking them to arrange themselves in the correct order in front of the class. As they hold the footstep signs in front of them, have the class read aloud each of the 5 steps in the decision-making process.

Based in part on a suggested activity in *Gerne, T.A. Jr. & Gerne, P.J. (1986). Substance Abuse Prevention Activities for Elementary Children. Englewood Cliffs, NJ: Prentice Hall, Inc.*

CLASSROOM GUIDANCE

ACTIVITY

TOPIC: Substance Awareness
TITLE: Facts and Myths About Smoking
LEVEL: 4th-5th
MATERIALS: Several smoking advertisements from popular magazines (choose ones that have a variety of surgeon general's warnings).

PROCEDURE: Begin by showing students each of the advertisements for cigarettes from popular magazines. Discuss with them what message the advertisement is trying to give the viewer. Point out that you never see an old, wrinkled, ugly model in these ads. Ask them if the stated or implied messages are true. Next, point out the white rectangle on the ad which contains the Surgeon General's Warning. Show examples of four or five different warnings. Note that prior to 1985, laws didn't require these warnings, but now they do...on cigarette packages and ads. Why?

Proceed to discuss the effects of smoking on a person's body. Ask if any of them have experienced these effects from being around a smoker. Discuss second-hand smoke.

Be sure to make the point that each person must decide for him/herself about smoking. They cannot make choices for their parents or others.

With the students' help, make two lists on board:

<u>Reasons to Smoke</u>　　　　<u>Reasons Not to Smoke</u>

Finally, ask which is the healthiest decision to make?　To smoke or not to smoke?

CLASSROOM GUIDANCE

ACTIVITY

TOPIC: Goal-Setting
LEVEL: 5th grade
MATERIALS: "Accomplishing My Goal" worksheet for each student, each of five criteria for goal-setting written on construction paper basketball cut-outs, interview questions written on strips of paper to hand out to a few students to ask wrestler, partner or student actor dressed up like a wrestler.

SET: Pre-arrange for a student to introduce "Big Risell" as the challenger to a well-known television wrestling personality. "Wrestler" enters and brags about his/her goal of winning the title next week. Counselor politely interrupts and asks: "Have you ever wrestled anyone before?" (no) "Well, 'Big Risell', it sounds like you may be setting yourself up to be disappointed. Let's look at some tips that may help you set a goal that you'll have a good chance of attaining.

PROCEDURE: Draw a basketball hoop on the chalkboard and ask students what it is. Say: "In order to reach a goal that we want to reach, there are 5 things to think about." Discuss each tip as you tape balls on board.

1) Is the goal specific?
2) Is it concrete?
3) Have you set a time frame for meeting your goal?
4) Can you attain the goal independent of anyone else's actions?
5) Is it a realistic goal for you given your past experiences?*

As you go over each step, have "Big Risell" respond. He/she should answer "no" to questions 4 and 5. Then tell him/her that it is important to set realistic goals so you can experience success. If you continue to set goals that are out of your reach, you will continue to fail and feel frustrated and disappointed. Can you think of another goal that you set for yourself and did reach?

Using this goal, go back over the steps it took to reach it. Then ask:
How did it feel to reach your goal? Do you have a new goal now?

Have students complete worksheet and share if time allows.

Interview questions for audience to ask wrestler:
• Do you have any experience in wrestling?
• Do you think you will win next week?
• How do you plan to defeat the champion?

ACCOMPLISHING MY GOAL

1. What is a goal I have?

   _____

   _____

2. What steps are needed to reach my goal?

   _____

   _____

   _____

   _____

3. What is a reasonable time in which to accomplish my goal?

   _____

4. I will keep going until I reach my goal or revise it.

5. I will evaluate and check my progress.

6. I will remember to compliment myself for progress made toward my goal.

Steps adapted from Project Self-Esteem by Sandy McDaniel and Peggy B Bielen, 1986.

Points to Remember
Chapter 6

1. Classroom guidance is the frame on which your entire guidance and counseling program is built.
2. Create lessons that actively involve students.
3. Classroom teachers should be asked to observe and follow-up on your lessons.
4. Counselors should not accept the role of "disciplinarian".
5. If you have a "runaway" classroom, utilize positive strategies, encouragement and rewards to motivate and maintain appropriate behavior.
6. Communicate your expectations clearly to teachers and students.
7. Mutual respect is the key.

CHAPTER 7

A Tour Through School-Wide Programs

The three main areas of responsibility for school counselors are counseling, consulting, and coordinating. We have talked about individual, small group and developmental counseling through classroom presentations. We have stressed the importance of maintaining good communication through regular consultation with teachers, parents, and administrators. The third area, coordinating, requires all the organizational and management skills you can muster.

Comprehensive guidance programs today are moving toward a large number of school-wide programs from drug abuse prevention to character education. Most of these programs necessitate many hours of planning and implementation by school counselors. If you don't see yourself as an organized person, you will learn to be. You will become much like a tour director who plans and works hard behind the scenes to insure a successful experience for his/her clients. In this chapter, I will tour you through a few of those programs. It is important to do a time-on-task analysis periodically to insure that you are balancing your time well. Almost all school-wide programs have meaningful objectives and are valuable additions to the school, but if not careful, you could find yourself spending all your time with them at the expense of direct student services. It will help if you have other staff members or volunteers to assist with some of these programs. If not, limit yourself to the most essential. It is better to do a few programs well, than to spread yourself too thin and feel unsuccessful at any of them.

New Student Orientation and Support

New student orientation is a vital part of my program. In our increasingly mobile society, it is not unusual for students to attend two or three schools in a year. We all know this can affect achievement and social adjustment. Some of the reasons students move or change schools are related to: divorce, remarriage, job change or unemployment, death, domestic violence, eviction, financial pressures, and others. All of these create a loss of some kind and may propel the student into the grief process. Counselor, student and teacher support can facilitate a smooth adjustment to these changes.

You may want to train "buddies" or peer helpers to guide new students through their first few days of routines and procedures. (For more information on training peer helpers refer to: Children Helping Children: Teaching Students to Become Friendly Helpers, Robert P. Myrick and Robert P. Bowman) I ask teachers to select one boy and one girl from their class to serve in this capacity. I meet with those students, give them badges, walk through their duties in September. I ask the school secretary in charge of registering new students to call the "Bee Buddy" from the designated class to the office to meet and escort the new student to class. Buddies are trained in introductions—-a skill often taken for granted by adults, but seldom practiced by children without prompting. They also give their new friend a welcome bag and a brief tour of the school.

On Friday of each week, I announce the names of new students and welcome them on our morning television program. The students are invited to the guidance office for a brief orientation session. This is a good time to learn names and assess the needs of each individual student. It allows the new student to meet the counselor and see his/her office as a welcoming place. Since these students have missed your beginning of school orientation, this is a good time to explain the self-referral process and your role in the school. I sometimes have students draw a picture of themselves to place on a bulletin board for new students. If your budget allows, Polaroid photographs may be used instead. (You can get two or three students in one picture.)

"NEW BEE IN THE HIVE" WELCOME BAG

We use quart-size ziploc® bags filled with:

- New student badge
- "Welcome to Flowertown" pencil
- "Busy Bee" sticker
- Bookmark (sample homemade one, or one from the library)
- Guidance brochure
- Booklet about our school
- Band Aid (from the nurse)

I get older students to help me prepare the bags and locate them in a basket in the office where all "BEE BUDDIES" can access them when they are called by the secretary to come greet a new student in their class.

FIGURE 7-1

Bee Buddies from: _____
(classroom)

Boy Buddy: _____

Girl Buddy: _____

Memo

To: Classroom Teachers Grades 1-5
From: Guidance
Date:
Subject: "New Bee Buddies"

This year we will again implement our "Bee Buddy" program to assist new students who come to Flowertown Elementary during the year. Because we're all new in a sense this year, we are a little late getting started. We ask that you select one boy and one girl from your class who may be "at risk" academically or environmentally, but who have satisfactory social skills. It could be a shy child or one who needs a boost in attention or self-esteem from accepting a small, but important leadership position in your class. "Bee Buddies" will be responsible for the following:

1. Helping prepare "new bee" packets (working with counselors).
2. Coming to the office to meet and greet the new student.
3. Giving the new student a "New Bee in the Hive" packet.
4. Assisting the new student with routines and procedures.
5. Introducing the new student to others in his/her class and/or pod.
6. In general, being a buddy for the first few days.

When a new student is assigned to your class, your "Bee Buddy" will be called to the office. Please have your buddy or buddies put on their badges (that you keep in a safe place in the classroom) prior to coming to the office. He/she will introduce himself/herself to the new student, get him/her a bag of welcome goodies (we will prepare and keep in the office), and return to the classroom. We ask that you allow the buddy to introduce the new student to you and the class. For that first day or so, the buddy should spend time with the new friend at recess, "show him/her the ropes" at lunch and in the classroom.

Since you will have a boy and a girl buddy, you may send the one that is the same gender as the new student, or send both if they would like. Some classes receive few new students during the year and the buddies all like the experience of doing their job as "Bee Buddy."

"Bee Buddies" will be trained by the counselors in small groups. We will announce new students and welcome them weekly on the intercom. Please listen for their names on Fridays and send them with buddies to our offices immediately following the morning announcements for an orientation session. Research shows that moving to a new school can be a very stressful experience for children (and teachers). We want to meet these youngsters early on, deal with the grief issues, and try to prevent problems in adjustment by working with them to help them fit in.

Feedback from teachers is that the "Bee Buddies" are extremely proud of themselves when they get to wear a badge and be in charge of "taking care" of a new student. It is our hope that self-esteem will be boosted for these children who otherwise might not get recognized.

Please submit your names by _____. We will notify you shortly thereafter of training times.

Thanks!!

FIGURE 7-3

CONGRATULATIONS

_____!

You have been chosen by your teacher to be a "BEE BUDDY." "Bee Buddies" are special students who are trained by our guidance counselors to assist in welcoming new students as they enter Flowertown. We realize that moving to a new school can sometimes be a difficult adjustment, and "Bee Buddies" can help make that adjustment as smooth as possible.

As a "Bee Buddy," you will be responsible for the following:
1. Helping counselors prepare "New Bee" packets as needed.
2. Coming to the office to meet and greet the new student. Introducing him/her to your teacher and classmates.
3. Giving the new student a welcome packet.
4. Assisting the new student with routines and procedures.
5. In general, being a "buddy" for the first few days.
6. Escorting the new student to a guidance orientation group on his/her first Friday. (Names will be called out during the morning announcements).

Thank you for helping with this important job.

_____
Your School Guidance Counselor

FIGURE 7-4

HELLO! I'm a new "bee" in the Flowertown hive.

This is my school.

Meet my new
teacher...

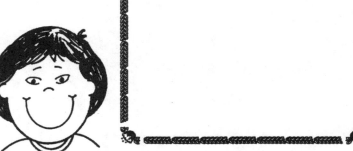

FIGURE 7-5

Look at all the fun things we do at school!

Something I like to learn about is:

_____.

Something I do well is:

_____.

Something that is hard for me is:

_____.

FIGURE 7-7

Welcome to Flowertown

New Bee in the Flowertown Hive

Draw yourself in the "bee plane."

State and District Testing Programs

Like it or not, school standardized testing programs are here to stay. Although requirements change from year to year and state to state, usually the school counselor is selected to coordinate these. (I guess it's because we're so organized and efficient.) At any rate, in my district, testing takes about a month in the spring...usually in April. Also, we coordinate first grade readiness testing the first three weeks each fall. Sometimes we help with testing for identifying talented and gifted students also. Whatever the case in your district, you will be trained at the local level by someone in the district office.

You will be responsible for teacher training, acquiring and assigning monitors, planning for alternate schedules on test days, enforcing security regulations and carrying out testing procedures in accordance with state and local guidelines. You will probably be responsible for disseminating test score reports when they arrive, and supervising the filing of reports in cumulative folders.

Because testing coordination requires a lot of time and focus, I have chosen to omit classroom guidance lessons for the month of spring testing. I miss seeing the students, but it is a trade-off I have found to be necessary to do a good job with testing and retain my sanity.

If you want to do test preparation activities with your students, a great source is Robert P. Bowman's Test Buster Pep Rally. It includes a potpourri of motivational activities to help prepare students for testing.

Be sure to thank teachers and monitors in some way for their cooperation with testing. Included in this chapter is a sample reward note with instructions about affixing candy, gum, and nuts that I have given to monitors after testing. A separate "thank you" would be appropriate for teachers.

FIGURE 7-8

THANKS _____ !

You were  nice

to help with _____ . (name of test)

You were a  .

Thanks a  (million!)

Without your help, we'd be...

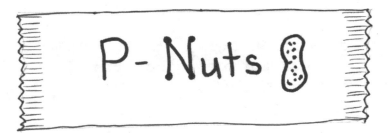

_____
Your Counselor

Substance Abuse Prevention Efforts

Federal money for "Drug-Free Schools" may be used in different ways. Our district has a district level program coordinator who works with a representative from each school. If you are the representative as I am, you will be responsible for coordinating efforts at the school level to promote substance awareness. This may include a prevention club and other school-wide celebrations.

These are some decisions that need to be made before beginning a prevention club.
1. What grade level/s will be included in the club?
2. Who will be the sponsor? Who will assist?
3. What type activities will you allow? (meetings, recess time activities, after school activities, pod activities, family outings, dances, food included, etc.)
4. What will be the goals of the club?
5. What times will be set for planning, communicating, and carrying out activities?
6. How will money be raised to support the club?

Beginning the club:
1. Decide on a T-shirt design. I had a contest among fifth grade students. The finished product was a combination of three of those ideas.
2. Announce the plans for time, place to join the club.
3. Send letter home to parents. Include T-shirt order form and purpose and plans for the club.
4. Schedule first meeting and initiation activity.
5. Have classes select Club Captains to help with sign-up duties and t-shirt sales. Meet with them to train.
6. Decide on membership cards, secret word, cheer and handshake if desired. Teach club captains.
7. Warning! Beware of Pothole # 9 SPEEDING in Heavy Traffic! Rushing into dozens of activities your first time out may jeopardize the success of your club and your well-being. Start out slowly and gradually add on new ideas.

I have included a sample parent letter and other forms I have used. Also, included is an outline of one substance awareness week agenda and sample activities and bulletin board.

FIGURE 7-9

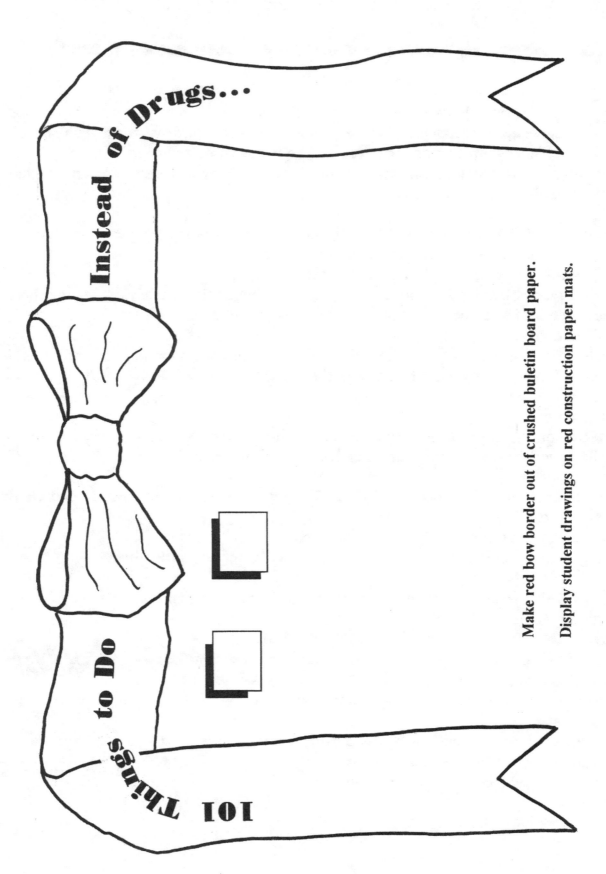

Make red bow border out of crushed buletin board paper.

Display student drawings on red construction paper mats.

FIGURE 7-10

"Bee" Healthy and Drug Free

I'm drug free so let me

Dear Parents,

During the month of January, we will be kicking-off Flowertown Elementary's "Just Say No" Club for students in grades two through five. Our guidance counselors will serve as club sponsors with the assistance of classroom teachers and student club captains from each class.

Our basic premise is "kids helping kids". Kids want their communities, homes, families, and themselves safe from the threat of alcohol and drug abuse and safe from negative peer pressure. We want to help our students learn about the risk associated with drug use and help them become better problem solvers. We will encourage students to unite in their efforts to support each other with positive peer pressure. We want to let kids know it's not necessary to use alcohol/drugs or to get into trouble to be "cool".

Club activities will include both fun and learning experiences. In-school activities will be held in classrooms, pod groups or assemblies. Also, we encourage family activities such as skate night. Watch for these announcements in the Flowertown Flier.

The club rules are simple:
1. Be the best you, you can be.
2. Help your friends resist negative peer pressure.
3. If you can't handle a problem, talk it over with an adult.
4. When you feel scared inside and suspect something is "wrong", "Just Say No".

There is no cost to join the club. All students will receive membership cards. T-shirts will be available for those who wish to purchase them for $5.25. If interested, complete and return the form below with payment. We are proud of our fifth grade student designers Harmony Rodrigues, Derek Nelson, and Kevin MacDonald whose ideas were merged to form the unique design on the following page.

Being in the "Just Say No" Club is sticking together, doing "stuff" together and helping each other to make good, safe decisions. We welcome your support and encouragement.

Sincerely,

Janet M. Bender
Shirley Kaasa

- -

I've read the letter about the "Just Say No" Club. My child, _____

in class section _____ wishes to order a t-shirt in the following size.
Payment of $5.25 is enclosed.

Youth size 10-12 (med.) _____   Adult size small _____
Youth size 14-16 (large) _____   Adult size medium _____   Adult size large _____

FIGURE 7-13

Flowertown Elementary
Just Say "No" to Drugs and Violence Club

Flowertown is organizing a club for all students in grades 2 -5 who are interested in saying "no" to the use of alcohol, drugs and violence. We need your help to select a slogan or motto for our club and design a T-shirt for our school club.

1. Choose a slogan. It may be original or one of the suggestions below.
2. Illustrate a T-shirt design in pencil. Outline in fine tip black pen.
3. Be sure to include school name and mascot (bee) in some way.

Possible Slogans:

Flowertown Bees Say "Buzz Off" to Drugs and Violence

Free to "Bee" Our Best...Without Drugs and Violence

Be the Best You Can "Bee"...Say "No" to Drugs and Violence

" Bee" Safe..."Bee" Healthy..."Bee" Drug Free...
Flowertown Says "No" to Drugs and Violence

Keep Peace in the Hive... Say "No" to Drugs and Violence

Flowertown Bees Take the Sting Out of Life...We Say "No" to Drugs and Violence

Your Slogan:_____

_____

Name:_____ **Class**:_____

Bender/1997

FIGURE 7-15

RED RIBBON WEEK
OCTOBER 24-30, 1997

SCHOOL- WIDE THEME: "Don't Bug Me, I'm Drug Free."

1) In <u>homeroom</u> classes on **Friday, October 24**, students will draw, color and cut out a bug of their choice. Students' names and sections should be on the back of the bug. We ask that these be collected and turned in to the PTA mailbox in the lounge before leaving on Friday. On Monday morning, PTA volunteers will help display all bugs around the school holding up a red ribbon.

2) **Library** will integrate the *Red Ribbon Story* into class lessons.

3) **Art** will assist students in each grade level with special projects.
   K-1st: Color sheets, thumbprints on posters with theme: "Bee Healthy and Drug Free."
   2nd-3rd: Design bookmarks with theme: "I'm Drug Free So Let Me Bee"
   4th: Design mini-posters with theme: "101 Things to Do Instead of Drugs"
        (Each student chooses one thing to be the focus of his/her poster.)
        These will be displayed on guidance hall bulletin board and around school.
   5th: Design T-Shirts for proposed "Just Say No to Drugs and Violence" Club

4) **P.E.** teachers will provide basketballs and playground balls with an anti-drug message for recess use. As always, they teach and encourage healthy use of leisure time.

5) **Music** classes will integrate appropriate self-esteem building selections.

6) **Classroom teachers** are encouraged to integrate drug awareness and Effective Communication (Strategies) activities into your health curriculum throughout the year.

DAILY EMPHASES:

Friday,   10-24-97- Kick off on WFES. Students create bugs in homeroom.
Monday, 10-27-97- All get red ribbons and stickers to wear throughout the week.
Tuesday, 10-28-97- Guidance "Bee Healthy" Tip and highlight of student work on WFES.
Wed.,   10-29-97- Wear Red Day
Thursday,10-30-97- Red Treat for Everyone Day

If you have questions or need assistance, ask Janet Bender or Freida Helmrich.

THANK YOU TO ALL THE VOLUNTEERS WHO HELPED PREPARE FOR THIS CELEBRATION!!

Parent Support

Parent support may come in the form of individual conferences and counseling sessions or with organized workshops or support groups. Additional support can be given through printed newsletters, handouts, or the lending of resources from your files or library of parenting materials. Connect with parents at every opportunity and let them know you appreciate their efforts and understand and respect the difficulty of their job.

Beware of sounding like you have all the answers... thus Pothole #10: KNOWING IT ALL. Whether you have successfully raised children of your own or not, you must remain ever so humble when sharing insights with parents. Try not to give unsolicited advise. When you do give advice, do it gently with phrases such as: Something that worked for me was... Maybe you could try... Would you like to borrow this book? You know your child best, but if it were my child I might try... I'm no psychologist, but... etc. Affirm the parent whenever possible and empathize with their frustration.

The guidance program in my district requires a minimum of two parent workshops each school year. If you are a new counselor, you may want to enlist a speaker from the community to do a workshop for you until you're ready to present on your own. Another option is to join forces with counselors from a neighboring school and plan a program together. This has worked well for me. After you've decided on a topic for a workshop or program, send out an attractive flier or pre-registration form to all parents. Experiment with times and topics for programs to discover which get the best turnout. If possible, draft teacher cadets or other volunteers to provide baby-sitting. This can be a headache, but it does increase the numbers of parents who participate. Try not to get discouraged if only a few parents show up. Some ideas for gaining parent involvement are:

1. Provide baby-sitting
2. Advertise
3. Make calls to invite targeted parents
4. Include children in some part of the workshop (peer mediator demonstration for program on conflict management)
5. Serve light refreshments
6. Make workshop fun and informative. Participants will spread the word to others.

FIGURE 7-16

COMING SOON!

...PARENTING PROGRAM...
"DISCIPLINE MAKES THE DIFFERENCE"
MARCH 4, 1997
7:00-8:00 pm
NES & FES GUIDANCE DEPTS
Newington Library

Learn:
... alternatives to yelling.
... to establish clear expectations.
... to use natural & logical consequences.
... behavior modification.
... time-out procedures.
... to deal with temper tantrums.

(Be a Better Parent in 60 Minutes!)

FIGURE 7-17

THE RESPONSIBILITY/SELF-ESTEEM CONNECTION

**How to Build
Your Child's Self-Esteem
Through Teaching Responsibility**

Monday, May 1, 1995, 7:00 pm
FLOWERTOWN LIBRARY

- -

```
I plan to attend the workshop,
"The Responsibility/Self-Esteem Connection"
on May 1 at 7:00.

Name/s_____

Phone _____ Child's name _____
```

Moving

Moving a few blocks away or across the continent...it doesn't seem to matter very much. To some children, moving presents a great new adventure, to others only an unwelcome upheaval of what is known and loved. To preschool children, a small move can be every bit as upsetting as a major one. Their geographical horizons are limited. If you're not allowed to cross the street alone, being told the new house is only a mile from the old one doesn't help. In such a case, children are not only leaving a familiar home and room, but are also leaving the yard, the corner park, the playmates next door. Moving diminishes a child's sense of being able to cope, and homesickness for the old environment may result.

It's a great temptation to farm out children to relatives or friends when the actual move takes place, but that temptation should be resisted. As in other or larger crises, participation helps children manage fears. They should go along on family trips to move fragile possessions. Even a young child can help pack his own belongings, being sure to leave a favorite night-time stuffed animal or blanket easily accessible. Distance allowing, the child should have visited the new house as often as possible and perhaps become acquainted with new neighbors. Helping to mend a fence or paint a room ahead of time will make the child feel more at home. If the new home is a great distance away, parents can use maps and photographs to introduce the child to the new home.

Late spring and summer seem to be favorite times for moving. For the sake of school-age children (even nursery school children), this timing may not be the best. In summer, family plans and summer activity schedules are already made, making it more difficult for the newcomer to edge in. And school, a good place to make friends, is not in session.

During the school year, classes, homework, and activities give the child something in common with new schoolmates. Many teachers and school guidance counselors know how to help the newcomer feel at home. Car pools, newly formed teams and clubs, and play groups help a new child join in.

Parents can help their children more directly, too, by joining family—-oriented organizations- such as community centers, Ys, churches, and temples—-where they will meet potential friends. Most communities need new leaders for Girl Scouts, Boy Scouts, Camp Fire Girls, little league or similar groups. Parents can help children fit in by becoming a leader of such a group.

As in other crises, family members should openly discuss their feelings about the move. Parents should be aware that their attitude toward the move will influence the child's opinion. It is normal to have some anxiety about change, but extreme negativism will only make the adjustment more difficult for everyone. To the school-age child who has not been doing well or has felt himself a loner in school, a move may appear to be a chance for a new start and be welcomed as such. Some experts think the shock can be softened by subscribing to the local newspaper a few months before the actual move. It will acquaint the family with what to expect, from grocery prices to movies, to family and youth activities.

(Source unknown)

How Parents Can Help When Children's Grades Are Poor

Interested parents are properly concerned when a child brings home poor grades or a bad report card. But what is the best way to react to the bad news?

"Being visibly upset and getting the child upset over the enormity of what he or she has supposedly done, is one of the worst possible reactions to poor grades," according to researchers at Stanford University in California. In fact, poorer grades are received by children of parents who express negative reactions to bad reports cards, and those students' grades are more likely to continue to decline.

Equally ineffective parental reactions include punishment, promising rewards for good grades, and no reaction at all.

What does work then? Research suggests that a low-key positive response—offering praise for the positive aspects of a child's performance, encouraging the child to do better with those things that aren't going so well, and offering to help, are the mostly effective parental responses to poor grades.

Beware of Haunted Houses!

As we approach the Halloween season, it seems an appropriate time to address my concern about the widespread acceptance of violent and horror-filled movies and videos as family c=viewing material.

As a school counselor, I work daily with children—some as young as five, who are either anxious and fearful, or intrigued and impressed—even humored by the on-screen displays of violence, blood, gore, monsters, bodily injury, bad people, guns, weapons, animals, bad dreams, being alone, getting lost or kidnapped, thunder and lightning, among others. Children in these formative years cannot be expected to absorb a steady diet of horror and violence in films without showing changes in their feelings, thoughts, and behaviors.

Children do not have the emotional maturity to screen out material that is not in their best interest. They depend on us as responsible adults to make tough decisions that protect them from unnecessary anxiety and fear and an unhealthy pre-occupation with special-effects violence—even if it means making them unhappy for the moment.

Please check ratings and preview questionable films and other experiences before allowing your children to view them. If your child sees and inappropriate adult film by accident, you can help him/her put it into perspective by discussing the content.

In today's world, there are enough real threats and anxieties for children to cope with without the added burden of self-induced fears through large doses of mur-derers, monsters, and violence. A "haunted house" used to be a make-believe, innocent, once-a-year experience for Halloween fun. Let's keep Halloween horrors from becoming a "haunting" year-long experience for our children.

(For more information on fears and stress in children, contact your child's guid-ance counselor.)

Role of the Elementary Counselor

As I was having my back adjusted on recent Friday afternoon, my chiropractor stated, "You don't have many problems to deal with in elementary school, do you?" His words motivated me to write this article about what elementary school counselors do.

School counselors teach life skills such as decision-making, team work, character education, self and career awareness to our 900 students. Through small group counseling we offer support, education and coping skills to students experiencing family changes, or other social/personal difficulties. We provide parent support and education through workshops, conferences, resources, and referrals. We coordinate many school-wide programs and clubs. School counselors listen a lot—to teachers, parents and students with concerns and burdens too heavy to carry alone. We intervene when necessary with students in crisis.

Yes, we do have problems in elementary school. our schools are an extension of our world. Our world is full of stress and chaos and the Nightly News follows students into the classroom. We do our best to make our school a supportive environment for learning and a safe haven from the cares of the world for a few hours each day.

School counselors, along with teachers, administrators, and other school staff, make a difference in the lives of youngsters. The difference is not always measurable by test scores, but it can be measured in the hearts and minds of our children. just ask them.

Sample Parent Letter

Dear Parent(s)/Guardian(s):

As a support to you and your child, I am enclosing some handouts pertinent to the topic we have been addressing in small group counseling. I have enjoyed working with your child. Please let me know if I can be of further assistance.

Sincerely,

Counselor

Conflict Management

At Flowertown Elementary, we have completed two years of a school-wide conflict management program. We selected Second Step (Pre-K) and Coping with Conflict, An Elementary Approach (1st-5th), as curriculum models for our program. Elements of program implementation have been:

1. Training for counselors, school staff and parents.
2. Teaching of skills through classroom guidance and supplementary teacher-taught lessons.
3. Periodic review of skills utilizing our WFES morning television program, parent newsletter articles, and teacher tips in mail boxes.
4. Reinforcement of skills through tangible rewards for students observed as "Care Bees," and school-wide recognition of appropriate behaviors through our "Caught Beeing Cool" program.

Peer Mediation "Bridge Builders" Program

There are many peer mediation/facilitator programs within schools which utilize trained student helpers to help other students resolve minor conflicts. This type of program is never a substitute for adult intervention and supervision of students, but can be valuable component of your school's conflict management program. Some possible goals and objectives of such a program are:

- To develop leadership skills among student facilitators.
- To provide appropriate student role-models for students who practice less appropriate social skills.
- To increase instructional time in the classroom by reducing teacher time spent on mediating minor student conflicts.
- To encourage and improve student communication and interaction skills.
- To promote honesty and respect among students.
- To improve problem-solving skills.
- To teach appropriate anger management strategies.

Getting Organized

At Flowertown, I began a peer helper program on a very small scale selecting, with the help of a fifth grade classroom teacher, eight students to train as facilitators. I went into the classroom and explained the responsibilities of a peer facilitator/friendly helper and left student invitations and applications with the teacher for interested students. Copies of those forms follow.

Students who were selected from the pool of applicants received a letter to take to their parents which included a schedule of training days and times. Parent and teacher approval were necessary criteria for participation.

With student input, we arrived at the name "Bridge Builders" for our peer facilitators. After successfully completing eight training sessions (or more if needed), students received badges and certificates.

The content of the training sessions will vary depending on the resources you choose to use in your school. However, thorough training should include: helper characteristics, feelings vocabulary, active listening, helpful responses, problem-solving model, positive feedback, and role-play. I have included samples of the handouts we used and the badge pattern I designed for peer facilitators.

The most challenging aspect of the peer mediator program for me was working out the logistics of when and where the mediation would take place. Time restrictions within the school day required sticking to a structured and limited block of time. Additionally, at the elementary level, adult supervision of the process is needed.

For more information on students helping students, read:

Myrick, R.P. & Bowman, R.P. (1991) Children Helping Children: Teaching Students to Become Friendly Helpers. Educationoal Media, MnMN.

The following forms include the student invitation and application for friendly helpers, student referral form, "Bridge Builder" agreement and badge pattern.

Student Invitation
for Peer Facilitator
(Friendly Helper)

Would you like to be a peer facilitator in our school? Peer facilitators work with other students. They are trained to be good listeners. They learn skills that they can use to help others talk about their ideas and feelings. Our peer facilitators will work closely with the counselors who coordinate this program.

A peer facilitator is a person who:

1. Is easy to get along with and who wants to help others.
2. Is caring and respectful of others.
3. Has a positive and cooperative attitude.

Responsibilities and helping projects may include:

1. Helping mediate minor student conflicts or concerns.
2. Being a peer tutor.
3. Assisting teachers and counselors.
4. Being available as a friend when another student wants to talk about something.
5. Assist with the fifth grade orientation program to middle school.
6. Helping make presentations to interested groups, such as local service clubs, parent groups, or school advisory groups.

Still interested? If so, complete the attached application form and turn it in to _____'s office. Final selections for this year's peer facilitator group will be based in teacher recommendations, parent approval and counselor selection.

Student Application
for Peer Facilitator
(Friendly Helper)

Student Name_____

Class _____Date _____

1. Why do you want to be a peer facilitator? _____

   _____

   _____

   _____

2. What skills or character traits do you have which would make you a good peer

   facilitator? _____

   _____

   _____

   _____

Teacher Recommendations/Comments:_____

   _____

   _____

Signature:_____

Parent Permission/ Signature: _____

Initial training will require meeting with the counselor **twice a week for four weeks.**
These meetings will be scheduled near the end of the school day at_____.
After training, the amount of time out of class will be limited in order to assure that
the students are able to maintain their academic responsibilities.

I Need To See
A Bridge Builder!

Name:_____

Class: _____Date: _____

Return this form to _____'s office.

Below this line is for guidance use only.

Did all persons agree to mediation? _____yes   _____no

Bridge Builders assigned: _____

_____

Mediation scheduled for:

Time: _____Date: _____

Bridge Builder Agreement

Date_____

I, _____, agree to work out my problem
with the help of a Bridge Builder. I am interested in resolving my problem.

I agree to the following:

1. I agree to tell the truth.
2. If I have a conflict with another person, I agree to listen to them without interrupting or name calling.
3. I agree to confidentiality (what is said here stays here).
4. I will respect the Bridge Builder.
5. I will control my anger.
6. I will do my best to brainstorm to find a solution and follow through with the final solution.

Signature:_____

Building a Bridge to Successful Resolution of a Conflict

I feel...

The reason is...

I want...

My understanding of you is...

Maybe we should try...

Let's choose & shake!

Maybe we should try...

My understanding of you is...

I want...

The reason is...

I feel...

Remember, that each time you find yourself in a conflict situation, you have the chance to build your own resolution bridge!

Take turns talking and listening to each other.

Adapted from several sources

"Caught Beeing Cool"

In the "Caught Beeing Cool" program, all teachers and staff members are provided with mini cut outs of green and yellow bees. As they catch a student practicing an appropriate skill for preventing conflict or using a tool they have learned for working out conflicts, they are complimented and given a bee. The student writes his name on the bee and places it on a huge beehive in the hallway. If he is lucky enough to receive a green bee, he immediately visits the treasure chest in the office as an additional reward. All bees on the hive are taken down at the end of each month and a drawing is held for "Cool Bee" t-shirts for a predetermined number of winners.

As you can imagine, the success of the program is determined by the degree of enthusiasm and ownership of the staff members. Counselors teach the lessons and conduct the follow-up reviews, but classroom teachers and administrators must motivate and reinforce the use of skills daily in order for it to be effective.

Another component we plan to introduce this year is a peer mediation program. There are many sources of information available for training peer mediators. Refer to the resource list at the end of this guide.

"Miss Manners" Contest

Another school-wide program that has helped motivate students to practice appropriate manners in the cafeteria is our "Miss Manners" program. Originated by my principal, the program enlisted the help of counselors, administrators, lunch room staff, and a few other selected teachers. Each of the six selected adults were assigned two weeks during the semester to act undercover as "Miss Manners." Our job was to secretly observe the grade level assigned to us in the cafeteria and select the class which exhibited good lunch room manners consistently. The criteria included eating quietly, respect for others and property, and basic table manners. The winning class each week was rewarded with a day of dining on the stage complete with table cloths, china, glasses, and service from cafeteria workers.

Since students did not know the identity of "Miss Manners," the anchor of our morning TV show kept their interest peeked by showing a different item each week that belonged to

"Miss Manners." A hat, pearls, high heels, white glove, fur collar, etc. were visual reminders of what to look for. On the final day of school, all six of us dressed up as "Miss Manners" and made an appearance on the morning show...each saying "I'm Miss Manners."

The principal solved the disagreement by announcing that we were all "Miss Manners," and that they would never know who would be watching them next year looking for their best manners. It was a fun and successful way to keep cafeteria behavior manageable.

Mentoring

Robert P. and Susan C. Bowman in their book, Becoming a Co-Pilot, A Handbook for Mentors of Children, define a mentor as "a person who gives extra attention and encouragement and communicates a deep belief in someone's potential." They remind us that many children today will not have this type of relationship occur naturally in their lives. Thus, we see an increasing movement toward school and community based mentoring programs.

Any caring adult with appropriate training can become an encourager to youth. But, a good program requires a lot of coordination, training and commitment.

Most programs that call themselves mentoring programs are well-meaning, but sometimes lack the organization and specialized training necessary to have a substantial and positive impact on the youth and the mentors.

I have only been involved in pseudo-mentoring programs in which school staff "adopted" at-risk students to spend special time with. We have also had "Papa Bees" commit to spending an hour a week with students in need. The most recent effort started at my school last year, was a program called "DADS," which was funded by a community grant and coordinated by individuals outside of the school. If you do decide to start a mentoring program make sure you include adequate training and supervision.

On a smaller scale, I have utilized older students within the school as friendly helpers for younger students. One successful effort included a play group where eight non-verbal first graders were paired up with older student friends for twelve weeks of small group activities which focused on developmental play activities such as finger games, songs, sculpting, art, drama, etc. At the end of the twelve weeks, the formerly non-verbal children performed a song and finger play for their homeroom class.

A sample program for this kind of mentoring is: Peer Pals! Kid's Helping Kids Succeed in School, by Robert P. Bowman, and John Chanaca.

Student Support Team

This team has many names and a variety of functions from school to school. It may also be called an Intervention Team, Pupil Response Service, Combination Team, or 504 Team. In any case, you will need to become familiar with the team at your school. In some cases, a counselor leads the team. The principal selects team members.

The purpose of our SST is to provide teachers with an avenue to express concerns about students who are not experiencing success in school and receive input from a multi-disciplinary group. The input might come in several forms:
1. Recommendations for changes in teaching strategies.
2. Recommendations for referrals to other sources such as medical, counseling, or 504 committee.
3. Ideas for behavioral interventions.
4. Recommendation to begin the psychological testing process.
   The team meets weekly throughout the school year.

Psychological Referrals

This is a process of evaluating students for possible learning problems. The counselor may be asked to coordinate the referral paperwork. This is a very time-consuming task. Special education staff members usually conduct the academic screening tests. Classroom teacher, speech pathologist, nurse, psychologist, and an administrator are all involved in this process. Check with other counselors or a district coordinator about the procedures they use.

Community Service Projects

Because of the flexibility of not having a homeroom, sometimes you will be asked to coordinate community service projects. Our school has committees assigned to these various duties. Two projects I have coordinated recently are a spring food drive and a secret Santa program at holiday time. Community service projects also qualify as school-to-work activities in the area of service learning. Individual classes, school clubs, and special education classes often take on service projects as well.

Spring Food Drive

I chaired a school committee which decided to conduct a food drive to support local charities. We used the theme: "Grow through Sharing." We made a hallway display including a large tulip flower for each grade level. At the base of each flower was a box covered to look like a flower pot. The stems "grew" taller each day as the canned goods added up. It was a friendly competition to see which grade could collect the most food items in a week. The visual display was also a lesson in graphing and a reminder of how well we were doing.

Secret Santa

For a number of years, our school has maintained a "Love Jar" fund where students drop their small change to be used for helping their fellow students in times of need. Sometimes, we buy shoes or school supplies for needy students. Sometimes, we decide on a school project such as helping flood victims. Usually the counselors coordinate getting referrals from teachers of students who need help at Christmas due to financial hardship in their families. We then shop, wrap and deliver to parents a gift of one clothing item and one toy for each child. Parents express appreciation and seem to be very grateful that the school cares enough to help out.

Celebrations/Events

Several times during the school year, you will have opportunities to coordinate or be involved with school-wide celebrations. Some of those might be:

1. National School Counseling Week
2. Career Day/Week
3. Child Abuse Prevention Month
4. Stop the Violence Week

My suggestion would be to choose one or two to emphasize heavily, then do a smaller celebration or recognition of the others. The American School Counseling Association provides celebration kits each year for a nominal fee which include ideas for celebrating around the theme of National School Counseling Week. A hall bulletin board is a good place to advertise special weeks and celebrations. I have included a sample bulletin board and an outline of sample activities for that week.

Career awareness should be an ongoing emphasis for all teachers. With the passing of the S.C. School-to-Work legislation in 1994, the movement in our district has been toward integration of the National Career Competencies into the curriculum. At the elementary level, our responsibility lies in the area of awareness. It is the responsibility of the counselor and school administrator to advise and train teachers of the legal regulations in regard to the law. Some schools still choose to hold a career day or week to highlight this area. However, this event alone does not satisfy the letter of the law in terms of career awareness. It is the responsibility of all teachers to help prepare students for the world of work by integrating competencies into their daily activities. In my district, Dorchester District 2, I facilitated the compilation of a School-to-Work manual, Focus on the Future, which gives an overview of ways we are meeting the needs of our students (K-12) in the area of career awareness, exploration and preparation. Additionally, the elementary counselors compiled and printed an activity resource book called Career Connections.

Child abuse prevention is an ongoing goal for all of us. Our local Exchange Club sponsors Child Abuse Prevention Month in April each year. They provide free materials to the schools upon request. Materials include brochures, activity ideas, blue ribbon lapel pins, and suggestions for educating the public on this important issue. The blue ribbon is their symbol, so all staff members are given a ribbon to wear during the month. Child safety lessons can be a part of classroom guidance this month. A bulletin board and table with handouts for parents is also a nice addition.

Stop the Violence Week is a new celebration started this past year. The local YWCA sponsors this emphasis. We integrate violence prevention into our "Just Say "No" to Drugs and Violence Club." A hall mural was displayed and students were encouraged to stop by and write anti-violence messages on it. Additional signs and posters were displayed throughout the school.

Many schools celebrate "Warm Fuzzy" Week or Random Acts of Kindness Week. These are both valuable concepts, but can be integrated into the classroom curriculum rather than singled out as a separate celebration if desired.

FIGURE 7-18

FIGURE 7-19

STOP THE VIOLENCE!

Violence Isn't Just Physical...

Emotional abuse, name-calling and yelling can hurt a person just as much as physical blows. Help "stop the violence" by stamping out sarcasm, mocking, teasing, yelling, stereotyping, gossiping, acting superior, and ridiculing.

Work for a peaceful school and community.

YWCA Nonviolence Day

©2003 YouthLight, Inc.

159

Other Miscellaneous Duties

In talking with other counselors, I have found that most have been assigned a few duties unrelated to their function as the school counselor. These duties include car and bus duty, breakfast duty, administration of screening tests, planning the master schedule, and a variety of clerical, supervisory, or administrative responsibilities. One counselor was even asked to sell popcorn on the playground. Several things to consider when assigned non-guidance duties are:

1. How much time does this take away from direct student services?
2. Does this duty create a conflict in roles? (disciplinarian)
3. Is this a responsibility that could be done quite well by a staff member with less specialized training than yourself?

I believe it is important to show that you are a team player by helping out whenever reasonable. If, however, the extra duties or responsibilities put unreasonable demands on your time, or create a conflict in roles with students, it is advisable to meet and discuss the situation with your principal.

There are many people in a school who are qualified to supervise students. You may be the only one on staff specifically trained to do counseling. Most principals are willing to listen and work out a compromise if approached professionally and tactfully. For example, one counselor was assigned morning bus duty which required being outdoors and unavailable to teachers and students for the first half hour of the school day. This is a prime time for consultation with parents, teachers and administrators. It is also an important time to be available to handle emergencies with arriving students. After discussing these points with her principal, she was allowed to trade duties and cover a dismissal duty instead. It wasn't a perfect solution, but it was a workable compromise. Knowing when to compromise and when to "draw the line" is a personal decision. As a last resort strategy, ask your principal to choose what guidance responsibility he/she wishes you to give up to make room for the added non-guidance duty.

My advice in these situations is to negotiate a compromise with your principal whenever possible. This is another time when your earlier work in public relations may pay off. If you have already proven your value to the school by staying busy and scheduling your time wisely, it will be much easier to sell your point of view.

Career Development

Career development falls into three distinct, yet overlapping areas: Awareness, Exploration, and Planning.* It is often the responsibility of the school counselor to coordinate these efforts. You may feel, like many counselors, that career development is a weak link in your total guidance program. My guess is that you have done more career awareness and development activities than you give yourself credit for. As you look over the twelve competencies which follow, notice that the topics of self-esteem, peer relations, decision-making and responsible work habits are among the national competencies. These topics have been addressed for years through classroom guidance activities. So, as you see, you already have a strong foundation on which to build.

On the national level, twelve career-related competencies have been identified. They differ slightly at the elementary, middle and secondary levels. It should be the goal of the educational system and the community to help students become better prepared for the world of work by developing these competencies through their school and home experiences. The school counselor cannot accomplish this task alone.

A part of the coordination effort of the school counselor is to educate others about their responsibilities in this area. The following diagram illustrates my interpretation of the integrated nature of the implementation of career development initiatives. A successful career development program must be integrated into all aspects of the school curriculum, as well as supported and encouraged in the home and community.

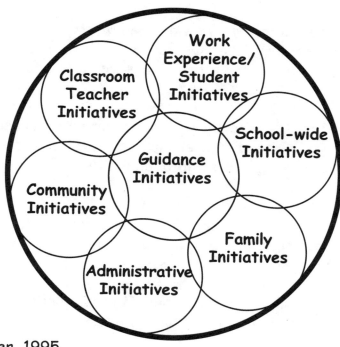

Janet Manning Bender, 1995

Faculty Inservice
School-to-Work Transition

This is a faculty presentation I gave in 1996 to introduce South Carolina's School-to-Work Act and educate teachers about their responsibilities in carrying out the regulations of that law.

You come here every day and "work your fingers to the bone," then go home and work some more to the point of exhaustion...only to turn on the nightly news or pick up the newspaper and hear the media say that we as educators are failing to do a good job. When I hear that, I get angry and I'm sure you do too. It's time to do what we learned in PET training and "work smarter, not harder." We're already working as hard as we humanly can.

What I'm going to say now may be hard for you to hear. But, I believe that **if** we've fallen short in doing our jobs of educating children, it's not because we haven't taught them lots of stuff, because we have. It **may** be because we have been preparing them more for **school** rather than for **life.** Think about it! Kindergarten teachers prepare children for first grade. First grade teachers prepare students for second grade. Second grade teachers prepare students for third grade. Upper elementary grades prepare students for middle school. Middle schools prepare them for high school and high schools prepare students for college. Employers are telling us that graduates are not prepared for the "world of work."

So, South Carolina has finally made a big step towards solving this problem through passing the School-to-Work Transition Act of 1994.

Today, I want to give you a brief overview of the law with emphasis on our part of the responsibility at the elementary level. Overall, I think we are already doing a pretty good job at this level, but there are a few things we can do to insure compliance with the law.

The bulk of the law impacts the secondary grades starting with record-keeping at grade six. Our primary responsibility at the elementary level consists of infusing career awareness and development activities into all subject areas grades kindergarten through fifth grade.

At this point, I showed a segment from a state video about the School-to-Work Act. Outside of SC, you may move on to the overhead of the twelve National Career Competencies and Indicators.

These are the 12 National Career Competencies. It is our goal to teach all students thee competencies by the time they graduate from high school.

DON'T PANIC! This looks like a lot to cover, and it is, but you do not do it all. It is a shared initiative by many groups which we'll look at in a minute. As we go over the competencies, I think you'll be relieved to find that we are already addressing many of them in our current program.

Briefly go over each of the 12 competencies. Then ask teachers to share which areas we (teachers and counselors) address on a regular basis. After some discussion, show overhead of "Building Blocks of Career Development." Point out where existing school instructional programs fit in.

In a developmental program, certain skills serve as the foundation for others to build upon. In the elementary years, we focus a lot on the areas in the bottom block of the steps. On the right, you see some examples of avenues in which these are taught. I'm sure you can think of additional avenues that you use in your classrooms. Notice as the blocks stack up, the competencies in the second level seem to be areas emphasized heavily at the middle school level and the top step at the high school level. We can teach any of them at any level, but it seems developmentally appropriate that mastery will follow a sequence similar to this.

Hold up a puzzle piece. Ask: What do I have here? By itself, one puzzle piece is pretty insignificant and unimportant, but how does a puzzle piece become important? When it finds its place among the other pieces to make a complete picture. You as a classroom teacher, are one important piece of the Career Development Puzzle.

The next overhead takes us "off the hook" in terms of shouldering the entire responsibility for preparing the children for the world of work. You can see the interlocking pieces which show many different audiences that are to share in the responsibility for implementing these career development initiatives.

For example: When holding attendance conferences with students and parents, an administrator can reinforce the concept that school is the student's job. This is a good opportunity to ask the child to infer the consequences of his /her behavior by asking him/her what would happen on the job if he were consistently late or absent. Administrator can affirm that in the real world, frequent tardiness or absence from work may lead to having one's pay docked, a bad evaluation, or maybe even to dismissal. Parents should be included as partners in the responsibility for getting young children to school regularly and promptly.

As a closing to this teacher training, and as an example of how one activity can encompass several competencies, I had teachers participate in an activity called Magic Carpet Ride into the Future. This is a classroom guidance activity in Chapter 6 of this book.

©2003 YouthLight, Inc.

Suggested Implementation of
Career Development Initiatives

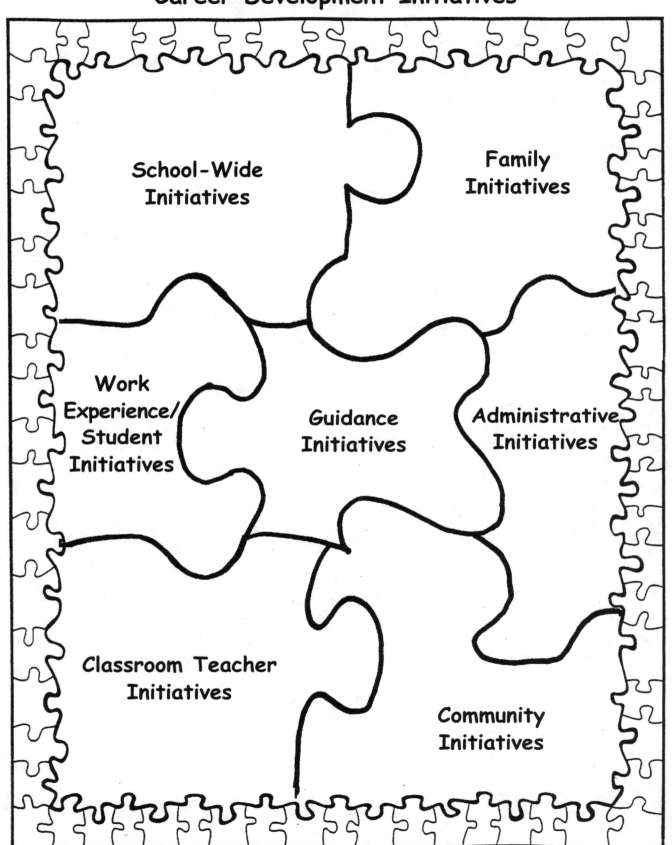

School-Wide
Initiatives

Family
Initiatives

Work
Experience/
Student
Initiatives

Guidance
Initiatives

Administrative
Initiatives

Classroom Teacher
Initiatives

Community
Initiatives

National Elementary
Career Development Competencies

Self-Knowledge

1. Knowledge of the importance of self-concept

2. Skills to interact with others

3. Awareness of the importance of growth and change

Educational & Occupational Exploration

4. Awareness of the benefits of educational achievement

5. Awareness of the relationship between work and learning

6. Skills to understand and use career information

7. Awareness of the importance of personal responsibility and good work habits

8. Awareness of how work relates to the needs and functions of society

Career Planning

9. Understanding how to make decisions

10. Awareness of the interrelationship of life roles

11. Awareness of different occupations and changing male/female roles

12. Awareness of the career planning process

As stated earlier, career development evolves through the elementary, middle and secondary levels with a focus on awareness, then exploration, and finally planning and application. I envision it as a structure of building blocks progressing through these stages and resulting in a finished product—-a student well prepared for the world of work. Career development does not begin in high school. It is the counselor's job to help educate the public (including your faculty and staff) about the importance of helping students see the connection between school and work from preschool through the high school years.

Building Blocks of Career Development

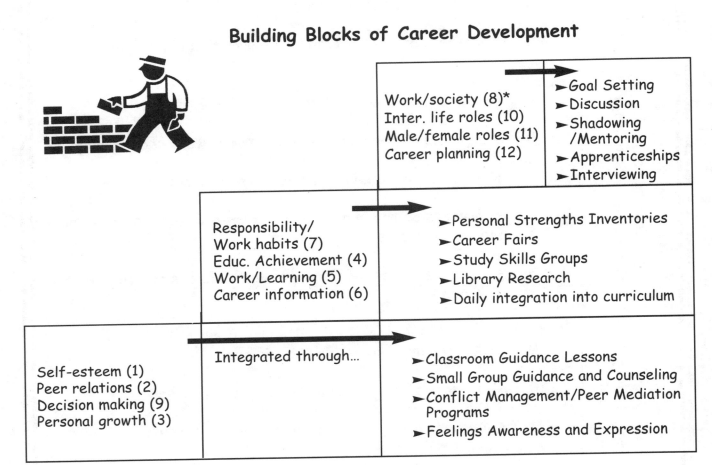

Work/society (8)*
Inter. life roles (10)
Male/female roles (11)
Career planning (12)

➤ Goal Setting
➤ Discussion
➤ Shadowing /Mentoring
➤ Apprenticeships
➤ Interviewing

Responsibility/
Work habits (7)
Educ. Achievement (4)
Work/Learning (5)
Career information (6)

➤ Personal Strengths Inventories
➤ Career Fairs
➤ Study Skills Groups
➤ Library Research
➤ Daily integration into curriculum

Self-esteem (1)
Peer relations (2)
Decision making (9)
Personal growth (3)

Integrated through...

➤ Classroom Guidance Lessons
➤ Small Group Guidance and Counseling
➤ Conflict Management/Peer Mediation Programs
➤ Feelings Awareness and Expression

* Numbers refer to the National Career Competencies. Suggested avenues for implementation

In South Carolina, legislators passed the School to Work Transition Act of 1994. In January of 1995, the SC State Board of Education provided school districts with guidelines for implementing the regulations required by the act. Of primary interest to school counselors is the section of the law concerning a comprehensive career development program. "A comprehensive career development program needs to be sequential. A program of activities should include career development activities that are infused into all subject areas in kindergarten through grade twelve utilizing state developed materials and/or commercially or locally developed materials/resources."

In the following pages, I have included a few career activities and resources that have been helpful to me.

©2003 YouthLight, Inc.

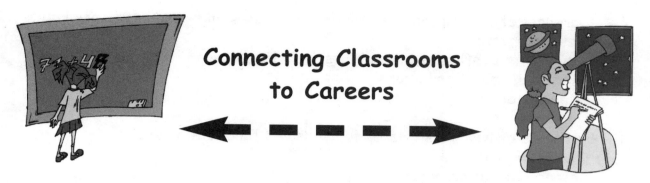

Connecting Classrooms to Careers

This outline may be helpful to classroom teachers who want to make a deliberate effort to teach career awareness/development, but aren't sure where to begin. It was provided by a second grade teacher who regularly integrates character education, life skills and conflict management into her presentation of academic subjects and daily classroom routines. The outline is organized by the 12 national elementary career competencies within the three major categories of career development (A,B,C).

A. Self-Knowledge

1. Knowledge of the importance of self-concept
   - School as job
   - Class rules are job expectations
   - Identify strengths, weaknesses and interests

2. Skills to interact with others
   - Coping with Conflict* skills provide tools for dealing with co-workers (other students.)
   - Lifeskills will enhance personal and interpersonal success

3. Awareness of the importance of growth and change
   - Ways to express feelings
   - Developing good health habits

B. Educational and Occupational Exploration

4. Awareness of the benefits of educational achievement
   - Good academic skills>good college/job>financial and personal success
   - Character Education and Lifeskills

5. Awareness of the relationship between work and learning
   - Classroom visitors describe job and skills needed to do job successfully

6. Skills to understand and use career information
   - Interviewing a person about his/her job/career
   - Role-playing jobs/careers
   - Writing about jobs/careers
   - Classroom jobs

7. Awareness of the importance of personal responsibility and good work habits
   • Listening posture
   • Coping with Conflict (Senn and Sitsch, 1998) skills
   • Character education lessons
   • Lifeskills booklet

8. Awareness of how work relates to needs and functions of society
   • Classroom visitors
   • Research about careers/jobs

C. Career Planning

9. Understanding how to make decisions
   • Conflict management skills
   • Character education
   • Role play decision-making and problem solving

10. Awareness of the interrelationship of life roles
    • Classroom jobs

11. Awareness of different occupations and changing male/female roles
    • Classroom visitors
    • Researching and writing about jobs/careers

12. Awareness of the career planning process
    • Reading and researching about jobs/careers
    • School as job>success in school leads to success in future job

* Source: C.B. Guess, "Classroom to Careers" presentation, 1999.

Career Awareness Bulletin Boards

Use colorful rainbow arches leading to a "pot of gold" to illustrate the path to a successful career.

Take photos of workers in the school including secretaries, teachers (art, PE, music, etc.) custodian, lunchroom workers, computer lab teacher, nurse, principal, media specialist, bus driver etc. Attach pictures to tree branches next to a symbolic picture of their job.

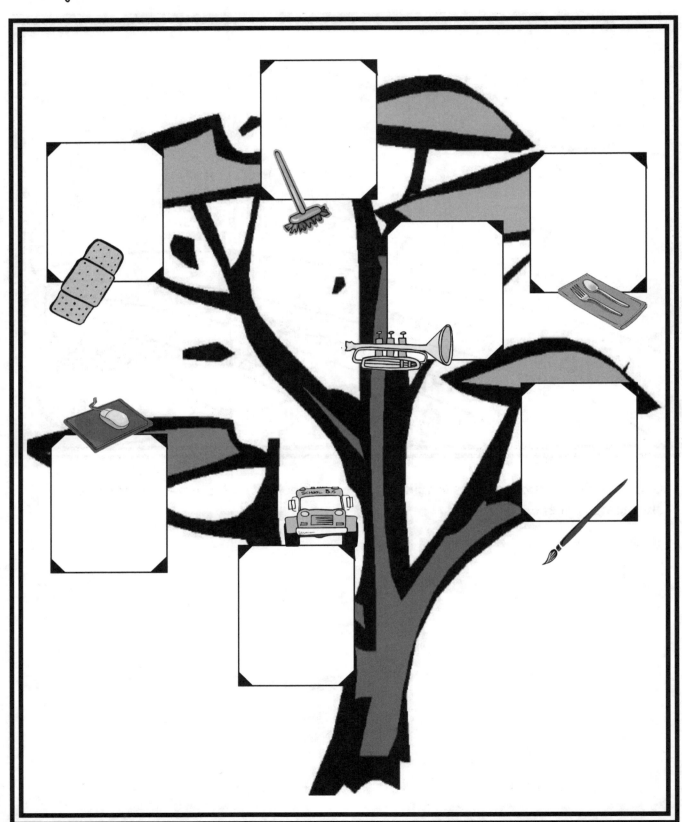

Suggested Career Awareness Activities

• Let students work with a partner to create a life-size "career paper doll." Have them research to find out what tools, clothes, etc. that worker uses and attach drawn "clothes, hats, tools."

• Invite a pool of speakers from the community into the school. After treating them to coffee and pastries, enlist the help of student council representatives from each classroom to escort a speaker to their class. After a designated time, (15-20 minutes) speakers return to central location and go with another student to a new class.

• Have a "Careers on Wheels" Day. Invite workers to school who use a vehicle in their job. Schedule classes to rotate around the parking lot or bus loop listening to each worker tell about his/her job.

• Invite students from a local vocational school to demonstrate some of the tools of their trade for students in their classrooms. In some cases, students can try on welding masks, hold tools, etc.

• Challenge students to write career poetry. Some state organizations sponsor contests with prizes to encourage student participation.

• Have students interview their parents or other adults they know about their jobs/careers.

• Encourage students to "shadow" an adult on the job on teacher work days.

• Use career-related topics for creative writing exercises for students.

• Survey faculty and staff about previous employment they have had. Use this information in morning announcements during Career Week. Example: "Guess who sold men's clothing and worked in a rubber band factory before he became a teacher?"

• Provide ideas to teachers for integrating career awareness into their daily curriculum. The following example is from a second grade teacher who did an excellent job of connecting classroom learning to careers.

• During American Education Week, invite school business partners to come talk to students about their businesses. Afterward, students will write stories or letters to be displayed at the business locations.

Recommended Resources for Elementary Career Development

Careers-Whole Language Theme Unit, K-1 (1993) Instructional Fair, Inc. Grand Rapids, MI.

Careers and Me, Primary (1995) Wintergreen/Orchard House Inc. New Orleans, LA.

Focus on the Future (1996) Dorchester School District Two, Summerville, SC

Occupational Outlook Handbook, Activites for Kids (1996) Wintergreen/Orchard House, Inc. New Orleans, LA.

Securing Futures: Guidance and Career Information (2000) Curriculum and Instructional Materials Center, Oklahoma Department of Career and Technical Education. Stillwater, OK.

The ABCs of the World of Work (1995) South Carolina Occupational Information Systems (SCOIS). Columbia, SC.

The Career Game (1997) Rick Trow Productions, Inc. New Hope, PA.

Thomas, Marlo (1972) Free to Be...You and Me (record and book).

* Carson Dellosa Publishers and Learning Tree are two other companies with a variety of career related materials.

Points to Remember
Chapter 7

1. The coordination of school-wide programs requires planning, organization and time management.
2. Start cautiously with one or two projects and proceed gradually into others.
3. Beware of SPEEDING into too many programs at once.
4. When offering support and counseling to parents, avoid KNOWING IT ALL behavior.
5. Get help from other school staff, committees, or PTA volunteers to assist with programs and celebrations.
6. Negotiate with your principal if assigned unreasonable non-guidance duties.

CHAPTER 8

A Pitstop
at the Rest Area
(Taking Care of the Caretaker)

Thus far, I have mentioned ten possible potholes to avoid as you embark on your new career as a school counselor. Following the suggestions in this guide can help you have a safe and enjoyable career journey. On the other hand, if you proceed too fast, too carelessly, or without direction, you may be headed for Pothole # 11, BURNOUT. In this final chapter, I offer ideas from my own experience to help you focus on those things within your control to maintain a healthy lifestyle while helping others.

Routine Preventive Maintenance

A human machine requires adequate service and maintenance to maintain good health while dealing with stress and daily routines. Do not wait until you are on the brink of a breakdown to begin taking care of yourself. Prevention is the operative word here. Getting adequate rest, good nutrition, time for recreation, and regular exercise can help. Additionally, self-renewal activities and relaxation practices will leave you better able to focus productively when you are at work. These are some pointers that have been helpful for me.

1. **Bed and Breakfast:** Eat nutritious, regular meals. Limit sugar, caffeine and alcohol. Don't skip meals. Get plenty of sleep...whatever that is for you. Begin and end your day with a meditation time focusing on inspirational, positive thoughts.

2. **Refuel Regularly:** Regular exercise...walking, weight training, aerobics, dancing, playing a sport, etc. even when you are tired, will actually give you more energy. It takes your mind off of daily responsibilities while giving your body a workout. Take time for fun and games that are not goal-oriented. Just play!

3. **Rest and Relax:** At least three times a week, try one of these or your own preferred R&R activity.

   Take a hot, soaking bath. Create a restful climate with candlelight and soft music. Put up a "Do Not Disturb" sign if necessary. Clear your brain of any thoughts other than the music and your breathing. (This won't be easy at first.)

   Practice deep square breathing. Breath in slowly on a count of five, hold for five, release for five, and rest for five, repeat several times. If you're used to a hurried lifestyle, (and who isn't?) you'll be surprised how hard this is at first, but it gets easier as you keep practicing.

   Learn and practice yoga.

   Read strictly for pleasure.

   Go to a concert, movie, ball game, or other spectator event.

   Play a board game or card game with someone you like.

   Get in touch with nature. Take a walk in a park or work in your yard or garden.

4. **Communicate:** Try writing in a journal...both the things that annoy you and those you are grateful for. Talk with a significant other about your frustrations and seek solutions together. If this person does not exist in you personal life, find a pastor or professional counselor. "Practice what you preach." Everyone needs to share important feelings with someone who cares. If you let tension build up by keeping it all inside, your relationships, your health and your job performance will suffer.

5. **Self-Renewal and Growth:** These activities can boost your performance like an oil change or tune-up does for your car.

> Take a course.
>
> Attend educational workshops.
>
> Visit other schools.
>
> Attend professional conferences and conventions.
>
> Travel.
>
> Engage in hobbies.
>
> Learn more about stress management and practice it.

Recognizing Detours

I have three files full of information on stress management, but I still struggle with it every day. Then I proceed to bash myself because "I should know better" than to let things get out of control. Precisely because you are in a helping profession, your personality is the type that is more vulnerable than some to burning out from giving too much. Recognizing the symptoms that lead to stress exhaustion can help you get back on track if you have detoured away from healthy living. Hopefully, you will learn to recognize them in time to set limits, organize your work and practice strategies to buffer the stress. The list on the following page is not original, but is from an anonymous source. Check the symptoms of stress exhaustion you've noticed in yourself lately.

FIGURE 8-1

Stress Exhaustion Symptoms

Physical

- ❑ appetite change
- ❑ headaches
- ❑ tension
- ❑ fatigue
- ❑ insomnia
- ❑ weight change
- ❑ colds
- ❑ muscle aches
- ❑ digestive upsets
- ❑ pounding heart
- ❑ accident prone
- ❑ teeth grinding
- ❑ rash
- ❑ restlessness
- ❑ foot tapping
- ❑ finger drumming
- ❑ increased alcohol, drug, tobacco use

Emotional

- ❑ anxiety
- ❑ frustration
- ❑ the "blues"
- ❑ mood swings
- ❑ bad temper
- ❑ nightmares
- ❑ crying spells
- ❑ irritability
- ❑ "no one cares"
- ❑ depression
- ❑ nervous laugh
- ❑ worrying
- ❑ easily discouraged
- ❑ little job energy

Mental

- ❑ forgetfulness
- ❑ dull senses
- ❑ poor concentration
- ❑ low productivity
- ❑ negative attitude
- ❑ confusion
- ❑ lethargy
- ❑ whirling mind
- ❑ no new ideas
- ❑ boredom
- ❑ spacing out
- ❑ negative self-talk

Spiritual

- ❑ emptiness
- ❑ loss of meaning
- ❑ doubt
- ❑ unforgiving
- ❑ martyrdom
- ❑ looking for magic
- ❑ loss of direction
- ❑ needing to "prove" self
- ❑ cynicism
- ❑ apathy

Relational

- ❑ isolation
- ❑ intolerance
- ❑ resentment
- ❑ loneliness
- ❑ lashing out
- ❑ hiding
- ❑ clamming up
- ❑ lowered sex drive
- ❑ nagging
- ❑ distrust
- ❑ fewer contacts with friends
- ❑ lack of intimacy
- ❑ using people

Source Unknown

Avoiding a Crash

Stress is a part of everyone's life. In small amounts it can even help you get the job done better and avoid procrastination. However, if you fail to take preventive measures, you may be vulnerable to a crash. The key is to remember that you are responsible to others for doing your best in this job, but you are not responsible for others, their feelings, opinions and behaviors. This final list of suggestions concerns on the job day-to-day performance.

1. **GET FOCUSED!** Spiritual and mental focusing through prayer or meditation can help you start your day on a positive note. Ask for guidance in using the knowledge and discernment you have been given to help others.

2. **PACE YOURSELF:** Slow down! If you're speeding at 90 miles per hour, chances are you'll end up "spinning your wheels," "going in circles," or "running out of gas." Check your walking, driving, and eating speed to measure your pace. Pace your self at a productive but not "breakneck" speed.

3. **TAKE TIME OUTS:** Just as sports teams need time outs to re-group and re-focus, so do you. Grab moments during your busy day wherever you can (in the bathroom, at a red light, lunch time) to pause for some deep breaths and positive self-talk.

4. **DROP EVERYTHING AND LEAVE:** Leave work on time or even early at least two days a week. Don't wait until you're totally stressed out or have a doctor appointment to take care of yourself. Do something for yourself...a walk in the park, an ice cream cone, extra time with your own children, etc. Believe me, that work will still be on your desk when you come in tomorrow.

Points to Remember
Chapter 8

1. Take care of yourself to avoid BURNOUT.
2. Prevent stress overload with adequate rest, good nutrition, and regular recreation and exercise.
3. Relax and do something for yourself at least three times a week.
4. Communicate with others.
5. Get involved in activities for growth and self-renewal.
6. Beware of detours that lead to stress exhaustion.
7. Stay focused.
8. Pace yourself.
9. Take time outs.
10. Leave work on time twice a week. If you get in the habit of staying late every day, others will begin to expect you to, and you may begin to feel guilty for leaving on time.

FIGURE 8-2

How to Love Yourself

1. **Stop all criticism**. Criticism never changes a thing. Refuse to criticize your self. Accept yourself exactly as you are. Everybody changes. When you criticize yourself, your changes are negative. When you approve of yourself, your changes are positive.

2. **Don't scare yourself**. Stop terrorizing yourself with your thoughts. It's a dreadful way to live. Find a mental image that gives you pleasure (yellow roses, etc.) and immediately switch your scary thought to a pleasurable thought.

3. **Be gentle and kind and patient to yourself**. Treat yourself as you would someone you really love.

4. **Be kind to your mind**. Self hatred is only hating your own thoughts. Instead of hating yourself, gently change your thoughts.

5. **Praise yourself**. Criticism breaks down the inner spirit. Praise builds it up. Praise yourself as much as you can. Tell yourself how well you are doing with every little thing.

6. **Support yourself**. Find ways to support yourself. Reach out to friends and allow them to help you. It is being strong to ask for help when you need it.

7. **Be loving to your negatives**. Acknowledge that you created them to fulfill a need. Now you are finding new, positive ways to fulfill those needs, so lovingly release the old negative patterns.

8. **Take care of your body**. Learn about nutrition and exercise. Cherish and revere the temple you live in.

9. **Mirror work**. Look into your eyes often. Express this growing sense of love you have for yourself. Forgive yourself looking into the mirror. Talk to your parents looking into the mirror and forgive them too. At least once a day, say: "I love you".

10. **Love yourself**. Begin it now. Do the best you can.

Have the courage to be imperfect and still love yourself!

Source Unknown

When I Feel Responsible For Others...

I fix:
- Protect
- Rescue
- Control
- Carry their feelings
- Don;t listen

I feel
- Tired
- Anxious
- Fearful
- Liable

I am concerned with:
- The solution
- Answers
- Circumstances
- Being right
- Details
- Performance

I am a manipulator.

I expect the person to live up to my expectations.

When I Feel Responsible TO Others...

I show
- empathy
- Encourage
- Share
- Confront
- Level
- Am sensitive
- Listen

I feel
- Relaxed
- Free
- Aware
- High self-esteem

I am concerned with:
- Relating person to person
- Feelings
- The person

I believe if I just share myself, the other person has enough to make it.

I am a helper-guide.

I expect the person to be responsible for himself and his own actions.

I can trust and let go.

Source: Hospice of Charleston

Potholes to Avoid

GOSSIP

ISOLATION

POOR COMMUNICATION

UNSTRUCTURED TIME

NO DOCUMENTATION

SPEEDING

DISCIPLINE

ENMESHMENT

KNOWING IT ALL

OVERLOAD

WARNING!
POTHOLE AHEAD

BURNOUT

Janet M. Bender, M.Ed., 2000

APPENDIX

This section contains additional lists and information referred to in the book.

➡ Review of Potholes

➡ Suggested List of Play Media

➡ Recommended Reading on Play Therapy

➡ Guidance Materials Inventory

➡ Resources & References

Review Of Potholes to Avoid for a Safe and Rewarding Career Journey

1. GOSSIP
2. ISOLATION
3. UNSTRUCTURED TIME
4. POOR COMMUNICATION
5. DISCIPLINE
6. NO DOCUMENTATION
7. OVERLOAD
8. ENMESHMENT
9. SPEEDING
10. KNOWING IT ALL
11. BURNOUT

SUGGESTED LIST OF ITEMS FOR PLAY AREA

The following is a list of basic toys and supplies for elementary school counselors.*

crayons,
newsprint
blunt scissors
plastic nursing bottle
rubber knife (clear with principal)

doll
Play-Doh®
dart gun
handcuffs
toy soldiers
play dishes
transportation/airplane, car, emergency vehicles
telephone
hand puppets/variety of characters from gentle to aggressive
bendable family dolls
doll house (a cardboard box with rooms indicated by strips of tape will also work)

doll house furniture
small plain mask (Lone Ranger type)
Nerf® ball
bendable Gumby® (nondescript figure)
craft sticks
pipe cleaners
pounding bench
old cap or hat
egg carton
inflatable punching toy

AVOID:
1. sharp, pointed, or glass items which could hurt a child;
2. elaborate, expensive, complicated or mechanical toys as they interfere with rather than facilitate, children's expression;
3. highly structured materials such as win/lose games because they do not promote creativity and exploration.

OTHER TOYS
magic wand, magic lamp
animals, domestic and wild
rubber snake
blocks
toy gun (if district policy allows)
camera
paints, markers
medical kit
mirror
sand tray, sand
miniatures for sand play (buildings, people, fences, trees, etc.)
tool set
foam bat and ball
baby blanket
small table and chairs set

You can purchase inexpensive Yaffa Blocks® and Rubbermaid® keepers and organizers to store and display toys.

Recommended by Dr. Garry Landreth, Handbook of Play Therapy. 1983, Edited by Schaefer and O'Conner

SUGGESTED PROFESSIONAL READING ON PLAY THERAPY

Gil, Eliana (1991) <u>The Healing Power of Play: Working With Abused Children</u>. New York: Guilford.

Landreth, Gary   (1991) <u>Play Therapy: The Art of the Relationship</u>. Munie, IN: Accelerated Development.

Schaefer, C. & O'Conner, K. (Eds.). (1982) <u>Handbook of Play Therapy</u>. New York: Wiley.

Axline, Virginia (1964) <u>Dibbs in Search of Self</u>. New York: Ballantine.

ELEMENTARY GUIDANCE MATERIALS

For a free catalog of other useful resources for Elementary School Counselors contact:

YouthLight, Inc.
P.O. Box 115
Chapin, SC 29036
(803) 345-1070 • (800) 209-9774
Fax (803) 345-0888 • Email YL@sc.rr.com
www.youthlight.com

RESOURCES AND REFERENCES

Blum, D.J. (1998). The School Counselor's Book of Lists. West Nyack, NY: The Center for Applied Research in Education.

Borba, M. & Borba, C. (1978). Self-Esteem: A Classroom Affair: 101 Ways to Help Children Like Themselves. San Francisco, CA: Harper.

Bowman, R.P. (1987). The Test Buster Pep Rally. Minneapolis, MN: Educational Media.

Bowman, R.P. & Bowman, S.C. (1997). Becoming a Co-Pilot: A Handbook for Mentors of Children. Chapin, SC: Youthlight, Inc.

Bowman, R.P. & Bowman, S.C. (1998). Individual Counseling Activities for Children K-6. Chapin, SC: Youthlight, Inc.

Bowman, R.P. & Chanaca, J.Jr. (1993). Peer Pals. Circle Pines, MN: American Guidance Services.

Foster, E.S. (1989). Energizers and Icebreakers. Minneapolis, MN: Educational Media Corp.

Forrest, D. (1998). 180 Days of Character. Chapin, SC: Youthlight, Inc.

Gerne, T.A. Jr. & Gerne, P.J. (1986). Substance Abuse Prevention Activities for Elementary Children. Englewood Cliffs, NJ: Prentice Hall, Inc.

Landy, L. (1984). Child Support Through Small Group Counseling. Charlotte, NC: KID-SRIGHTS

La Rock's Fun and Magic Outlet. Charlotte, NC: (704) 563-9300.

Myrick, R.P. & Bowman, R.P. (1991). Children Helping Children: Teaching Students to Become Friendly Helpers. Spring Valley, CA: Jalmar Press.

Schmidt, J.J. (1991). A Survival Guide for the Elementary/Middle School Counselor. W.Nyack, NY: The Center for Applied Research in Education, Inc.

Senn, D.S. & Sitsch, G.M. (1996). Coping With Conflict: An Elementary Approach. Chapin, SC: Youthlight, Inc.

Starr, M. F., & Gysbers, N. C. (1997). Missouri comprehensive guidance: A model for program devvelopment, implementation and evaluation (1997 Rev.). Jefferson City: Missouri Department of Elementary and Secondary Education.

PARENTING MATERIALS:

Successful Parenting video series. Active Parenting, Atlanta, GA.
Canter, L. & Canter, M. (1985). Assertive Discipline for Parents,
Conter & Associates, Inc. Harper & Row.
Quick Communications for Parents, P.O. Box 27891, St. louis, MO:
63146

This list is just a part of the inventory in my office. There are many more excellent materials available.